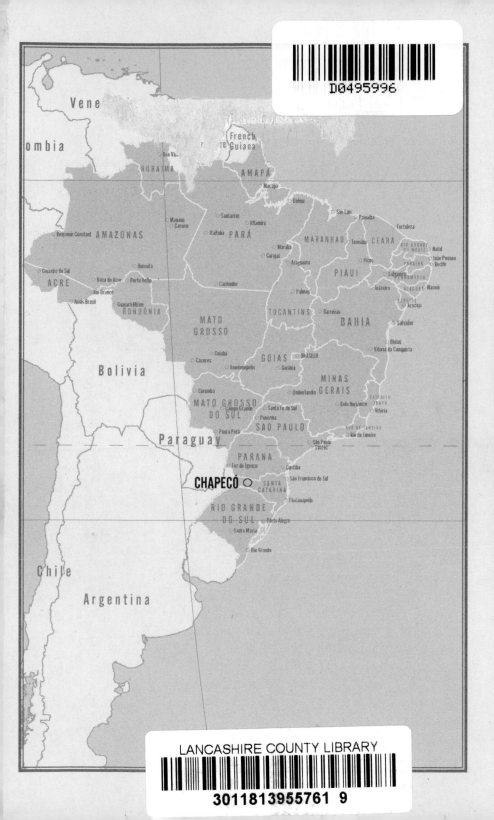

FROM TRIUMPH TO TRAGEDY

FROM TRIUMPH
TO TRAGEDY

THE CHAPECOENSE STORY

S T E V E N   B E L L

Assisted by Sergio MF Valeriano

First published by Pitch Publishing, 2019

Pitch Publishing
A2 Yeoman Gate
Yeoman Way
Worthing
Sussex
BN13 3QZ
www.pitchpublishing.co.uk
info@pitchpublishing.co.uk

ISBN 978 1 78531 523 7

Typesetting and origination by Pitch Publishing
Printed and bound in India by Replika Press Pvt. Ltd.

Contents

'Ali começava, uma linda história.
Que a mensagem deixada por eles
sirva para que todos nós,
valorizemos cada dia e que us
boas lembranças não desapareçam de
nossas memórias.'

'It began there, a beautiful story.
May the message left by them be
for us to value each day,
and for us not to allow good
memories to disappear.'

Two-time Chapecoense head coach
Vinícius Eutropio to the author;
5 February 2019

Dedicated to:

Luiz Carlos Salori
Eduardo de Castro Filho
Anderson Rodrigues Paixão Araújo
Anderson Roberto Martins
Marcio Bestene Koury
Rafael Correa Gobbato
Luiz Cesar Martins Cunha
Luiz Felipe Grohs
Sergio Luis Ferreira de Jesus
Anderson Donizette Lucas
Adriano Wulff Bitencourt
Cleberson Fernando da Silva
Emerson Fabio Di Domenico
Eduardo Luiz Preuss
Mauro Luiz Stumpf
Sandro Luiz Pallaoro
Nislon Folle Junior
Decio Sebastião Burtet Filho
Jandir Bordignon
Gilberto Pace Thomas
Mauro Dal Bello
Edir Félix de Marco
Davi Barela Dávi
Ricardo Philippi Porto
Delfim Pádua Peixoto Filho
Marcos Danilo Padilha
Ananias Eloi Castro Monteiro
Arthur Brasiliano Maia
Bruno Rangel Domingues
Ailton Cesar Junior Alves da Silva
Cléber Santana Loureiro
Dener Assunção Braz
Filipe José Machado
José Gildeixon Clemente de Paiva
Guilherme Gimenez de Souza
Everton Kempes dos Santos Gonçalves

Lucas Gomes da Silva
Matheus Bitencourt da Silva
Sergio Manoel Barbosa Santos
Willian Thiego de Jesus
Tiago da Rocha Vieira
Josimar Rosado da Silva Tavares
Marcelo Augusto Mathias da Silva
Mateus Lucena dos Santos
Victorino Miranda Chermont
Rodrigo Santana Gonçalves
Devair Paschoalon
Lilacio Pereira Junior
Paulo Julio Morales Clement
Mário Sérgio Pontes de Paiva
Guilherme Marques
Ari de Araujo Junior
Guilherme Laars
Giovane Klein Victória
Bruno Mauro da Silva
Djalma Araujo Neto
Andre Luis Goulart Podiacki
Laion Machado Espíndola
Renan Carlos Agnolin
Fernando Schardong
Edson Luiz Ebeliny
Gelson Gailotto
Douglas Dorneles
Jacir Biavatti
Over Goytia
Sisy Arias
Romel Vacaflores
Alex Quispe
Gustavo Encina
Angel Lugo
and Miguel Quiroga

Introdução

In the summer of 2014, I spent six weeks in Brazil as they hosted their beloved FIFA World Cup.

In that time, I developed a fondness for the country: for its people, for its football, for its passion.

On my return, I kept in touch with one particular friend I had made there and I began to loosely follow their politics and, even more so, their football.

Like most of my smart-phone-enslaved generation, my first act of a morning is to look at the time on my iPhone. The brightness always feels harsh to the blurred, barely open eyes, but we all do it regardless, every day.

During the working week, I will cancel the alarm that is emanating from the device and then spend around ten minutes checking the social media, news and sport applications for any breaking stories whilst my mind catches up to my eyes in the waking process.

Occasionally, something newsworthy will have happened in the time zones of the Americas, and my BBC News application will have sent an alert to my device, showing me the headline on the home screen as I cancel the audible alarm.

If there has been a large sporting event in the US overnight, my Sky Sports application will do the same, sometimes ruining the result for me if I am hoping to catch up with the event later in my own time.

In November of 2016, with the US election victory of Donald Trump sensationally secured, it was becoming the norm to wake with a BBC News alert displayed. They usually informed me of the latest outrageous and potentially world-peace-damaging tweet the president elect had made.

On the morning of Tuesday, 29 November, I had slept at the house of my then girlfriend, now wife, Nicky. I remember it well, as we had been celebrating the one-year anniversary of our first date. On waking, my straining eyes and barely cognitive brain saw that something had happened on the other side of the Atlantic Ocean that had made both BBC News and Sky Sports send me the headline bulletin.

The plane transporting the Brazilian football club Chapecoense to the biggest match in their history had crashed. I was very much aware of 'Chape' (pronounced Shar–pay) following their rapid rise to prominence.

As the hours went on, I checked various news outlets for the latest on the accident. There were mixed reports on casualties and on what had actually happened.

Within a couple of days, the full extent of the tragedy had emerged and the story was major news here in the UK, and the world over. *#ForçaChape* (#BeStrongChape) was trending worldwide for a week or two as the biggest stars from football and beyond, all around the world, paid tribute.

After two to three weeks, there was no more coverage of the story in the British media. We were back to the same news coverage as before, dominated almost entirely by Donald Trump and Brexit.

But my interest had been peaked almost to obsession by the event. Everything I read on the subject just made me search for more information.

I began to believe it was possibly the greatest sporting story of them all and became frustrated that it seemed to be cared about and known of so little, even amongst football fanatics in the UK and beyond. So, I decided I would attempt to fulfil the lifelong ambition of writing a book, in a bid to bring the tale to the fore in the English language.

Prólogo

Perder, Ganhar, Viver

Written by Carlos Drummond de Andrade, who is considered one of the greatest ever Brazilian poets, following the elimination of the national football team from the 1982 World Cup at the hands of Italy.

Translated from Portuguese to English by Eric M. B. Becker.

Lose, Win, Live

I saw people crying in the streets when the referee blew the final whistle that sealed our defeat;

I saw men and women full of hate trampling yellow and green pieces of plastic that only minutes earlier they'd considered sacred;

I saw inconsolable drunks who couldn't understand why their drinks brought no consolation;

I saw boys and girls celebrating the defeat so as not to fail to celebrate something, their hearts wired for joy;

I saw the team's tireless, stubborn coach called a lowlife and then burned in effigy, while the player whose many shots missed wide of the goal was declared the ultimate traitor to his country;

I saw the news about the man who killed himself in the state of Ceará and the death of hope in many others on account of this sporting failure;

I saw the distress of the upper middle class dissolved in Scotch whisky and, for the same reason, heard deafening cries from children mired in despair;

I saw a young man change his tone, accusing his girl of being a jinx;

I saw the stifled disappointment of the president, who, as the country's number one fan, had been preparing for a moment of great personal and national euphoria, after the many disillusions of his government; I saw candidates from the incumbent party stunned at the bad luck that robbed them of a powerful triumph for the campaign trail;

I saw the divided opposition parties united by perplexity in the face of a catastrophe that could bring voters to lose enthusiasm for everything, including the elections;

I saw the anguish of the makers and sellers of tiny Brazilian flags, pennants, and various symbols of the highly coveted and widely demanded title of four-time world champions now headed, ironically, for the wastebasket;

I saw the sadness of street sweepers and maids in apartment buildings as they wiped clean the remains of a hope now extinguished;

I saw so many things, I felt so much in every soul...

I'm arriving at the conclusion that defeat, which always catches us unawares in our desire to avoid it and inability to accept it, is, in the end, a means toward renewal. Like victory, it establishes the dialectic game of life. If a series of defeats is crushing, a series of wins plants the seed of our determination's decay, a post-conquest languor that paralyses once vital individuals and communities. Losing implies the shedding of dead weight: a new beginning.

Certainly, we did everything we could to win this fickle World Cup. But is it enough to give one's all and then demand fortune deliver an ironclad result? Wouldn't it make more sense to attribute the ability to transform things and invalidate the most scientific of conclusions to chance, to the imponderable, even to the absurd?

If our team only went to Spain, the land of mythic castles, to bring a cup back in a suitcase as the exclusive and inalienable property of Brazil, what merit is there in this? In reality, we went to Spain due to a love of the uncertain, of the difficult, of imagination, and of risk—not to nab a stolen prize.

The truth is we haven't come home empty-handed simply because we didn't bring back the trophy. We returned with a tangible good, a mastery of the spirit of competition. We vanquished four equally ambitious squads and lost to the fifth. Italy had no obligation to roll over in the face of our genius on the pitch. In a battle of equals, fate's gaze passed us over. Patience—let's not transform a single experience, amid many, of life's volatility into a national crisis.

In losing, after the tear-soaked emotionalism has passed, we reacquire (or acquire, in the case of most) a sense of moderation, of a reality full of contradictions but also rich in possibilities, life as it truly is. We're not invincible. But we're also not a bunch of poor wretches destined never to reach greatness, that most relative of values with its tendency to go up in smoke.

I'd like to pat the heads of Telê Santana and his players, his second- and third-stringers, like the unplayed journeyman Roberto Dinamite and to tell them with this gesture what with words alone would be a bit silly and overblown. But this gesture is worth a thousand words, we can feel its tenderness. Oh, Telê! Oh, athletes! Oh, fate! The '82 Cup has come to an end, but the world has not. Neither has Brazil, with all of its ills and its blessings. And there's a brilliant sun outside, a sun that belongs to all of us.

And so, dear fans, what do you think about getting to work now that the year's half over?

1
17th July 1994

The Rose Bowl
Pasadena
Los Angeles

It is the biggest and most important football match in the history of the sport.

A crowd of 94,194 screaming supporters are crammed into the huge, iconic stadium. It's almost 30 degrees Celsius in California as the players of Italy and Brazil are led out onto the pitch. The two superpowers of international soccer, joint record holders with three World Cup titles each already, will battle it out for glory and a history-making fourth championship.

It is Europe versus South America. It is the *Azzurri* (Blues) against the *Canarinhos* (Little Canaries). It is the infamous Italian defensive rock taking on the legendary Brazilian attacking flair. Or at least that *should* be the case. But this Brazil team is different. To the displeasure of the obsessive supporters and the media in his home country, coach, or *técnico*, Carlos Alberto Parreira has somewhat abandoned the long-held principles of '*O Jogo Bonito*'– 'the Beautiful Game' – in favour of a pragmatic approach more akin to the Italian way.

Following a long, glory-filled spell where 'The Samba-Boys' had taken the sport to new heights in terms of flair and entertainment on the pitch whilst dominating the World Cup, picking up the Jules Rimet Trophy three times between 1958 and 1970, a barren spell had been suffered.

Parreira had watched closely as manager of lowly Kuwait in the 1982 tournament, held in Spain, when a golden generation of Brazilian talent was left heartbroken as they crashed out of the *Copa do Mundo* the world expected them to win, with a squad of brilliantly flamboyant attacking players such as Serginho, Socrates and Zico.

But in the second round they had met a team willing to sit back and frustrate them: to foul them, to counter-attack, to hope their star striker would punish them with a clinical finish. That player was Paolo Rossi. That team was Italy. Rossi scored all three goals for the *Azzurri* as they eliminated the tournament favourites by three goals to two.

The loss was nothing short of traumatic for the whole nation, and to exacerbate the pain Italy went on to their third tournament victory, tying the Brazilian record that had stood for 12 years. They did so by scoring just 12 goals in their seven tournament matches, whereas the Brazilian swashbuckling style had plundered 15 goals in only five games before their premature elimination. Yet it was Italy that held the trophy aloft.

The legendary Pelé, widely regarded as the greatest footballer of all time and star player in each of the three *Canarinhos* tournament victories to date, had coined the phrase '*O Jogo Bonito*', which became the informal term translated worldwide for football played with flair and skill; 'the Beautiful Game'.

Now, in 1994, with a less skilled pool of talent to choose from, Parreira has developed a more pragmatic style similar to that of the European nations, especially Italy. They rely heavily on star *atacante* Romario to score the vital goals whilst the defensive unit remain militant and organised, and he is not disappointing. He has scored five goals en route to this centrepiece finale.

The newly installed style of play has worked thus far, as Brazil's presence in the final confirms. But the supporters and media are still critical and using this tactic against the masters of it is surely suicidal. Franco Baresi and Paolo Maldini have a combined total of 138 international appearances and are an almost impenetrable central defensive partnership for Italy; they will surely limit the goalscoring chances of Romario even more.

At the opposite end of their team, they have Roberto Baggio. Known as '*Il Divin Cordino*' (the Divine Ponytail) due to his trademark hairstyle, graceful style of play and Buddhist beliefs, Baggio is officially the greatest, having been voted the 1993 World Player of the Year. Italy have scraped through all three of their knockout matches so far, winning by two goals to one in each of them. Baggio has scored five of those six goals, two of them in the final moments of their respective matches with his nation on the verge of elimination. Their reliance on his attacking prowess is immeasurable.

The diminutive pair of superstars, Romario and Baggio, are also going head to head for the lucrative individual tournament awards of top goalscorer and best player. Brazil have only ever known one way to play the game their nation is besotted with, to attack with pace and skill and to entertain their loyal supporters. Far removed from the Italian style of refining and glorifying the 'dark arts' of the game, defenders in Brazil are mostly failed attackers, and the goalkeepers failed defenders. Luckily for this generation though, a rarity historically for them, the *Canarinhos* have a specialist *goleiro*, in the shape of the balding and pale-skinned 28-year-old, Claudio Taffarel. He is not only of Italian descent but plays his domestic football in the famous Italian league for Reggiana. The São Paulo press had launched a campaign to get their goalkeeper, Zetti, to replace Taffarel, but Parreira has stood firm with his favoured number one.

With the sport ingrained in their respective cultures, the two nations have come to a total standstill for this most epic and historic of encounters.

Approximately ten per cent of the whole world's population is tuning in on TV screens around the globe.

The match gets underway and, predictably, wave after wave of Brazilian attacks are dealt with by the solid Italian defence. Whenever Italy do manage a counter-attack, the incomparable Taffarel is equal to any danger. Half-time comes and goes. Minute piles upon minute as the pressure builds.

Italian goalkeeper Gianluca Pagliuca shows signs of the palpable tension as he clumsily deals with a comfortable-looking long-range shot from Mauro Silva, the world gasping as he spills the ball around the post. Silva is partnering his captain Dunga in the middle of midfield. They are of little footballing skill, but are strong, brave and energetic. Polar opposite to their 1982 counterparts Zico and Falcao.

Hungarian referee Sándor Puhl blows his whistle, bringing an end to the scheduled 90 minutes, signifying an extra 30 be played in the baking heat, which is sapping the physical and mental energy of the glory-seeking players.

At the age of 34, Franco Baresi has been inspired in defence for his nation. He has covered every blade of grass in the Rose Bowl in his quest to become the first non-Brazilian to win two World Cup medals (14 individuals of the legendary Brazil generation won back-to-back titles in 1958 and 1962), having tasted glory in the 1982 tournament in Spain. But his body is beginning to let him down after almost two hours of arduous perfection.

Both Bebeto and Romario finally manage to find themselves with glorious opportunities, but fail to convert.

Baresi's body screeches to a halt as he becomes paralysed with cramp and is forced off the pitch on a stretcher. Italy, having already made the maximum two substitutes, will be forced to see out the final moments with one player less on the field.

With mere seconds remaining, it looks as though the script has been written by the footballing gods as Baggio makes an attempt from distance with a typically sublime shot, but yet again Taffarel makes an impressive stop.

Another blow of the whistle from the referee signifies the players' and fans' worst nightmare: a penalty shoot-out will decide the most important moment in the history of this, if not any, sport.

The two teams will take five 'spot-kicks' each. Whoever converts the most takes home the ultimate prize. Every heartbeat can be heard and felt in Brazil as their fate is close to being decided. Will it be a repeat of the nationwide depression of 1982, or redemption over the Italians and glory once again? Repeat, or redemption?

It is Italy to shoot first and to everyone's shock, team captain Baresi returns to the field of play to assume the responsibility. He is facing Taffarel, who is known as a penalty-saving specialist and has the added advantage of knowing his opponents' penalty-taking styles all too well from his weekly appearances in their domestic league.

As Baresi strikes the ball, his failing body collapses backwards, propelling the ball into the air, way over the goal structure and into the stands behind. He falls to his knees with emotion. He is distraught.

Brazilian defender Marcio Santos approaches in expectation of consolidating the advantage for his desperate nation. But Pagliuca reads the kick and dives to his right, blocking the shot. It is now three hours since the match started, and still the teams are locked in a goalless stalemate.

But that swiftly changes as the *Azzurri* midfielders Demetrio Albertini and Alberigo Evani and the *Canarinhos* stars Romario and Branco convert successfully.

Next up for Italy is Daniele Massaro. A dropped pin could be heard amongst the almost 100,000-strong crowd. Taffarel knowingly predicts where the ball is going, dives to his left and parries it away from goal. Legendary commentator Galvão Bueno screams with delight: *'Vai que é sua, Taffarel!'* over the Brazilian airwaves. He repeats this phrase over and over, which translates to mean 'Go for it, Taffarel, make it yours!'

Once again glory is within their grasp, and inspirational captain Dunga steps up to confirm the advantage, and he converts the kick with typical authority.

With the score at three goals to two in favour of Brazil, the pressure mounts firmly on the shoulders of the world's greatest football player. *Il Divin Cordino* Roberto Baggio has to score or the tournament is over.

He faces the inspired and heroic Taffarel. He knows he has to strike firmly and accurately to beat this man. In his graceful, almost lazy-looking style, he jogs towards the target, strikes the ball on its underside and the shot follows an almost identical flight path to that of his captain, Baresi, as it continues to rise and carries over the goal into the stands.

Redemption.

A whole nation cheers as 200 million people cry tears of joy.

The men in yellow celebrate the historic victory and find enough energy in their sapped bodies to race towards their hero Taffarel.

It is the elusive and fabled *'Tetracampeonato'* they had prayed would eventually come. The fourth championship.

But for the first time their hero, alongside *atacante* Romario, is their *goleiro*.

A Triumph.

2

Campeões Eternos

Wild celebrations ensued all across Brazil following the summer World Cup glory of 1994. It had been 24 years since the population of over 200 million had seen their adored heroes thrust the trophy aloft and hold the title of world champions that meant so much to them.

The phrase '*Vai que é sua, Taffarel*' became a national symbol of bravery, joy and victory and was soon being used in everyday life. For the first time, schoolchildren wanted to be a heroic *goleiro* so that their name would be yelled as part of the iconic catchphrase.

The country suffers from political unrest and corruption, from social and economic inequality. Football is the only common denominator between the citizens, regardless of age, gender, wealth or social standing.

Brazil was the final country in the Western world to abolish slavery. By the time it stopped in 1888, an estimated four million slaves had been imported from Africa, which makes up around 40 per cent of the amount brought to the whole of the Americas.

Unlike most countries, following abolition, the slaves were not given any support. The legacy of this is such that more than a century later the vast slum areas, known as *favelas*, are occupied almost entirely by Brazilians of African descent.

Almost 25 per cent of the population live below the poverty line, with more than 50 million Brazilians belonging to families with an income of less than US$6 per day (all figures given using 2017 statistics).

The richest one per cent (approximately two million people) take 13 per cent of all household income. The poorest 50 per cent, around 100 million, share the same percentage of earnings.

This is perpetuated by the poor standard of state education. The higher earners send their children to private schools, but the poor are forced to go through the low-level public system, which limits their chances of social mobility via an academic route. They cannot realistically become doctors or lawyers, architects or engineers.

But they can become footballers.

The *futebol* system, however, mirrors the inequality of the economy. The hierarchical structure hosts around 30,000 professional players across approximately 1,000 teams.

All these teams play in their respective state championships, of which there are 26. These State *Campeonatos* run during the first four months of the calendar year.

Following this the national '*Brasileiro*' pyramid structure begins and runs from May to December. Only 60 of the 1,000 teams are assured of a place in the national leagues. A further 68 can qualify by a good performance in their state championship; the rest are forced to close their gates for the remainder of the year. Many players are released into obscurity at this stage. The lucky 68 clubs are the ones which perform best in the top tier of their state championship, but who are not already part of the top 60. Confusing, I know.

At the peak of the national pyramid are 20 teams that compete each year in *Série A*, the premier division. Here, players regularly perform in front of crowds 50,000-strong and earn riches up to $100,000 per month playing for the most prestigious and historic clubs such as Flamengo, Santos, Corinthians Paulista and São Paulo.

For many of the teams though, these riches can be short-lived as they constantly battle '*rebaixamento*', which means demotion to the next level down, *Série B*. The bottom four clubs in *Série A* exchange places with the top four teams in *Série B* every year. This jeopardy system continues to the very bottom of the hierarchy, where players don't get paid at all and are forced to play on dry, dusty fields in front of crowds of just dozens.

In *Série B*, players can earn up to $5,000 per month and provide an excellent standard of living for themselves and their families.

Going down to the third tier, yet another selection of teams make up the final truly national division, *Série C*. Here players can earn up to a respectable $2,000 per month.

Below this, *Série D* is made up of the 68 qualifying teams split into regional divisions. For a team outside *Série A, B* or *C*, the only hope of making it is to perform exceptionally in their state championship and make it into the top four (out of 68!) to make the automatic jump to *Série C*. All this has to be achieved in the same year.

If a club falls below the top tier of its respective state championship, it is in a complete wilderness as the route back to the national divisions is so far and the revenue so small. Many teams go out of business if this happens.

Série D was incepted for the 2009 season; previous to this *Série C* was of a similar format but following this became the third truly national league.

Almost all the players at this level, making up 84 per cent of the total number of professional footballers in Brazil, earn less than $500 per month and most are paid the minimum wage, which is less than $300. They live in poverty. Most are forced to give up the game early to work as refuse collectors, road sweepers and market traders to earn more money and to provide for their families. And the cycle continues as their children cannot go to the private football schools, but are forced to play barefoot on the hot, dusty streets and parks. The lucky ones who live in coastal regions get to hone their skills on the beach. Players that break from this cycle into the upper echelons of the sport are rare.

There are levels even above that of *Série A*, where the best performing teams go on to play in the South American international club competitions, *Copa Libertadores* and *Copa Sul Americana*, which are the equivalent of the Champions League and Europe League in Europe, respectively. The governing body of South American football is CONMEBOL, equivalent to Europe's UEFA.

The elite Brazilian players, especially the ones that achieve their dreams of pulling on the *Canarinhos* jersey, are usually signed up by clubs in the super-rich European leagues. Claudio Taffarel played in Italy, superstar Romario performed for the iconic FC Barcelona in the Spanish league. And as of 17 July 1994, these were no longer just inspirational heroes to a whole generation of poverty-stricken children in Brazil, but they were also *campeões eternos* – eternal champions – who brought home the coveted trophy for the first time in their young lives. They provided hope of a better future, one that included glory and adoration. They were *deuses*; they were gods.

The supporters were so deliriously happy they had forgiven Parreira for his negative tactics. The scathing press had been forced to completely reverse their narrative of him as he became a national hero for delivering '*Tetracampeonato*'.

Parreira, just like many of the players, took advantage of the worldwide notoriety he had received and went to the riches of European football, becoming coach of Valencia in Spain. Despite leaving his post, his philosophy of playing purely for results regardless of how gritty and defensive the style of play may be, continued in Brazilian football. It was '*Era Parreira*' as they went in search of '*Pentacampeonato*', a fifth World Cup triumph.

Iit was either triumph or tragedy for Brazilian football. There was no in between.

3

Pentacampeonato

Celebrating on the pitch that sunny Sunday at the Rose Bowl was 17-year-old striker Ronaldo Luis Nazario de Lima, known simply as Ronaldo.

He had been included in the squad after a blistering start to professional football in the *Brasileiro,* scoring 44 goals in 47 games for Cruzeiro of *Série A*, which had seen him and his team win the *Copa do Brasil* and their State Championship, the *Campeonato Mineiro.*

He was a non-playing member of Parreira's squad, having been brought along as a fourth-choice *atacante* but also as a mentee of Romario, with the assumption he was the heir apparent to the throne as the *Canarinhos* superstar forward.

Romario, before moving to Barcelona in 1993, had spent five years playing for Dutch side PSV Eindhoven and was held in high regard at the club. He was so impressed with Ronaldo within the squad of the 1994 *Copa do Mundo* that he advised PSV to purchase the youngster, which they subsequently did.

Ronaldo was a revelation in Europe. He was the top goalscorer in Holland in his first season at just 18 years old and went on to spend two seasons there, scoring 54 goals in 58 matches. The football world now stood to attention and he was dubbed 'O Fenomeno' (the Phenomenon).

FC Barcelona parted with a then world-record transfer fee of $19.5 million for his services. In his first season, the 1996/97 campaign, Ronaldo plundered 47 goals in 49 matches. He was now a worldwide superstar and his goal celebration of running along the adoring fans with his arms outstretched in homage to Christ the Redeemer, the famous religious statue which looks over his native Rio de Janeiro, was the image on the front and back pages of newspapers around the globe.

He was instantly recognisable, with his dark skin tone, shaven head and trademark protruding front teeth, which he showed off constantly as he smiled and laughed whilst setting new records and standards of play within the sport.

At just 20 years of age, he won the FIFA World Player of the Year award and after only one season in Spain, Ronaldo broke his own transfer record when Italian giants Internazionale paid $27 million for him.

Ronaldo continued to amaze in Italy, the league best known for the skill of the defenders. He was now a muscular man of 21. Opposition players that could get close to him, if he hadn't beaten them with a piece of ball skill or blistering speed, would simply bounce off his athletic frame.

For his native Brazil, Ronaldo and his mentor, Romario, had combined to form a fearsome duo which had become known as the *Ro-Ro* attack. In 1997 alone the pair scored a combined 34 goals for their country. In 1998 Brazil would be defending their crown as France hosted the latest edition of the tournament that meant so much to so many in their homeland. The pair were expected to blast Brazil to '*Pentacampeonato*', a fifth crown.

'This is very sad for me, a big disappointment. This is a very difficult moment in my life.' A sobbing Romario had to give a press conference explaining that he had picked up an injury, while back playing for his boyhood club in Rio de Janeiro: Vasco de Gama. He would be absent from the tournament. But, Brazil still had the all-conquering Ronaldo, who seemed to have reached a physical peak at such a young age.

They were now back under the tutelage of the legendary Mario Zagallo, who had won the World Cup twice as a player and once as the coach in the '58, '62 and '70 tournaments respectively.

On 12 July 1998, Brazil would take on host nation France in Paris in the final of the *Copa do Mundo*. Ronaldo had done his duty, scoring four goals en route whilst the defenders behind him continued to hold a tight line, as per the tactics installed by Parreira four years previous. France, meanwhile, had stumbled to the final, needing extra time to get past Paraguay, penalties to see off Italy and having to come back from a goal behind to beat Croatia 2–1 in the semi-final.

A video clip emerged of the French defenders in training before the final. They were preparing for coming up against Ronaldo, admitting when he is on form, nothing could be done. Lilian Thuram and Marcel Desailly had played against him in the Italian league. 'Whether he goes left or right, you don't see the ball!' says Desailly, as he mimics the two feet of Ronaldo in front of him. 'Where is the ball? It's magic!'

The final would take place at the Stade de France in Paris. Once again, the whole world stopped for the mouthwatering clash; 72 minutes before the game was due to get underway the team sheets were entered by the managers of the respective teams. Shockingly, Ronaldo was omitted from the paper Zagallo handed to the officials. News of this leaked out to the media and a storm erupted and wild theories began. Was it the niggling ankle injury that he had been nursing? Was it a reoccurrence of the knee injury that had blighted him before? Rumours emerged of a stomach bug. If this was true, could it have been a deliberate act? They were going against a home nation looking for their first ever title after all.

Soon, a revised team sheet was hurriedly put forward just before the one-hour deadline, on which the superstar name returned. The mayhem and questions did not stop though.

Ronaldo was virtually non-existent in the match, in which a Zinedine Zidane-inspired France won by three goals to nil. As it became apparent Ronaldo was no threat, *Les Blues* pushed further and further up field and put the Brazil back-line under the type of pressure it hadn't come against before, and it cracked.

It emerged later that Ronaldo had suffered a convulsive fit in the hours leading up to kick-off. Zagallo knew he was not fit to play but caved under the pressure of the storm that brewed from his original team entry, and apparent pressure from the player himself. Zagallo had wanted to replace him for the whole of the first half, but feared a public outcry if he had.

Once again, the pressure of the Brazilian population and media had been to the detriment of the team.

For the first time, more members of the squad were based in Europe than in the *Brasileiro*; this also caused unease amongst the football-crazed supporters, as they felt their national team was being taken away from them.

But the overall performance had been very positive and Brazil knew it would only be a matter of time before the trophy was back on their shores for the record-breaking fifth time.

Brazil's fans had also seen the graceful skill on the world stage of another brilliant attacking player who was already the latest in the line of Brazilian stars to ply their trade at the Nou Camp stadium, Barcelona. His name was Rivaldo and he went on to win the 1999 World Player of the Year award. Tall, with broad shoulders, a shaven head and a muscular physique, he was the opposite type of player to what his appearance would first make one assume. Poised, graceful and elegant, his performance had reached new levels in his late twenties.

This period also saw the emergence of a precociously talented youngster from Porto Alegre – Ronaldinho – who, after impressing for Grêmio in the *Brasileiro*, got his big-money move to Europe when Paris Saint Germain paid $5 million for his signature. He was a throwback to the legendary skilled footballers the country had produced half a century beforehand; those who honed their skills on the beaches and on the dusty streets and played because it was fun. All the time on and off the pitch, a beaming smile would light up his face, with his cartoon-like front teeth unmistakeable as his curly black hair bounced around. Given the choice of an easy pass to a team-mate or an attempt to bamboozle the opposition with an outrageous piece of skill, Ronaldinho would always choose the latter, to the delight of his supporters.

In 2002, the World Cup would travel east for the first time as Japan and South Korea combined as hosts for the tournament.

Romario was now 35 years old and although he was still scoring goals aplenty in the *Brasileiro*, there were question marks over his attitude and commitment. Brazilian superstars who come from the poverty-stricken streets and *favelas* tend to have relatively short careers at the very top level as the types of food, drink and all manner of other possible vices they could only dream of being able to afford are now readily available with their riches.

Romario was a true legend in his country but sentiment would not play a part in the selection of new *técnico* Luiz Felipe Scolari. Romario was omitted in favour of the attacking trio of Ronaldo, Rivaldo and Ronaldinho.

Going into the tournament, they were the most feared team in the history of international football. 'Big Phil' as Scolari became known in the English-speaking press due to his large frame, had happened upon another golden generation. One with the same flair and skill the public so desperately wanted but also one that, due to the legacy of *Era Parreira*, had the defensive and tactical abilities to compete with the modern European ways.

They swept all before them in the group stage and the first knockout round, against Belgium. Then came the quarter-final match-up against England, who were proud to be fielding a golden generation of their own featuring David Beckham, Paul Scholes, Rio Ferdinand and, at the time, European Footballer of the Year Michael Owen. Many believed the winner of this match would go on to win the whole tournament.

After 22 minutes of play, a mistake by the *Canarinhos* defender Lúcio gave the predatory Owen a chance, and he made no mistake. Against the odds, England had the lead.

As the half-time whistle approached, playing added time after the opening 45 minutes, Ronaldinho drove at the England players down the centre of the pitch and one by one they committed themselves as the mercurial 22-year-old jinked left and right. He left the defenders strewn on the floor and, as he bore down on the final one, he instinctively knew Rivaldo was now clear to his right. He dropped his shoulder left, successfully taking the final defender with him and subsequently creating even more space for his team-mate, and simultaneously tapped the ball right where the awaiting Rivaldo coolly and effortlessly swept the ball past goalkeeper David Seaman. It was 1–1 at the interval, but the timing of the goal had an ominous feeling for England.

Early in the second half, Brazil, playing in their changed blue strip, were awarded a free kick. It was 40 yards out and at a wide angle to the goal. Ronaldinho stood over the ball as the offensive and defensive lines of players waited on the edge of the penalty area for the aerial delivery. Seaman stood five yards from his line, hoping to be the first to the ball, to pluck it from the air with his gloved hands.

In a World Cup moment that will last forever in the memory of supporters, Ronaldinho struck a curling ball high and powerfully into the air, looping it over the head of Seaman into the top corner of the goal. The ball dropped inches below the crossbar and inches above the outstretched glove of the goalkeeper.

A forlorn England never looked dangerous from that point on and the two moments of genius from Ronaldinho had settled the epic encounter.

A semi-final against over-achieving Turkey was settled by a single Ronaldo goal to set up a classic World Cup Final of Brazil versus Germany, who were also alongside Italy on three previous titles and therefore had the opportunity to draw level with Brazil on the record of four.

In truth, this wasn't a vintage German team. Their goalkeeper Oliver Kahn won the Player of the Tournament award after saving his team game after game.

After a nervous opening, the final was a little bit of an anti-climax, another two Ronaldo second-half goals predictably and decisively delivering '*Pentacampeonato*'. Once more, the huge population of Brazil could enjoy the title they live and breathe for: football world champions.

A closer study of the tournament only proves further just how good this generation was: they scored 18 goals in the finals and conceded only three. The now legendary attacking trio scored 15 of the 18 goals, eight going to 25-year-old Ronaldo, who had played in his third *Copa do Mundo* Final, and but for an ill-timed seizure, may well have celebrated a win in all three.

Brazil appeared to be set for another extended era of dominance.

The press and public were ecstatic; the 24-year drought now a horrible but distant memory. Next up in 2006, the host nation of the tournament was to be the very same nation the *Canarinhos* had just brushed aside in the final. Surely it would be title number six, '*Hexacampeonato*'?

4

Chapecó

'OUR SQUAD SHOWS COMPLETE APATHY AND SAYS GOODBYE GLOOMILY TO THE WORLD', read the depressive headline in the Brazilian number one newspaper *O Globo* on the morning of 2 July 2006.

In a repeat of the *Canarinhos'* last defeat in a *Copa do Mundo* tournament, elimination had come at the hands of France. A single goal by Thierry Henry saw the defending champions sent home early from the tournament in the quarter-final, the earliest stage they had exited since the 1990 showpiece in Italy, 16 years previous.

As was the usual thing to do after conquering the mountain of winning a World Cup under the immense pressure of 200 million expectant supporters and the scrutiny of the baying press, Scolari had stepped down after the 2002 tournament. His replacement was none other than Carlos Alberto Parreira. This time, his overly defensive tactics had failed. *Era Parreira* appeared to have begun with him at the helm and now finished as such, as the press got their revenge for 1994 when he proved them so wrong. This time around, he left his position under a dark cloud.

He had picked an ageing squad with an average age of almost 30, and deployed them in a similar manner to 12 years beforehand. Typifying the problem with doing this was the right-back position, where Cafu, now 36, was playing, just as he had in 1994.

Football had evolved in that 12 years, and the Parreira tactics now looked out of touch, and the press ensured he knew it. Once again, he left his post after the tournament, this time in shame rather than glory.

In 2002, 12 of the 23-strong World Cup finals squad had been playing in the *Brasileiro*. In the 1994 and 1998 edition of the tournament that number had been 11 and nine respectively, out of 22-man squads. Only three of the failed 2006 contingent played their domestic football in the *Brasileiro*; all the remaining 20 were now plying their trade in Europe.

Following the phenomenal 2002 performance, a Brazilian international footballer was the top commodity in world football and the wealthy clubs of Spain, Italy, England and Germany took many of the stars purely based on their association with the successful tournament. This was causing a feeling of disconnection between the adoring public and the team. The only time they got to see their heroes was in the golden yellow jersey and if they individually or collectively had a poor performance, the inevitable accusation was that they cared more about the foreign clubs lavishing them with extraordinary salaries whilst the average supporter back in their native country was still living in poverty.

Rivaldo had finished his international career three years earlier but the emergence of Kaká, who had already secured his passage to the European major leagues with AC Milan, was seen to have filled the void more than adequately. At the same age as Kaká and also playing in Milan, but for rivals Internazionale, was Adriano, an aggressive but skilled attacker who had been in the best form of his career leading up to the tournament.

With this pair joining Ronaldo and Ronaldinho, it was thought *O Jogo Bonito* would return.

The quartet turned out to be a huge disappointment.

The powers of Ronaldo, now approaching this 30th birthday, were clearly waning. He was playing and still scoring regularly for Spanish giants Real Madrid but was spending a lot of the time on the sidelines with various injuries and was struggling to keep down his weight and remain the first-class athlete he had been. At the tournament he was the target of jeering from opposition supporters about his physical shape, but still managed three goals to take his overall World Cup tournament tally to 15, a record at the time.

Conversely, Ronaldinho had developed his career: after becoming the latest Brazilian superstar to transfer to Barcelona in a $30 million deal, he had been named FIFA World Player of the Year for two years running prior to the tournament and was putting pressure on the upper limits of any football ever seen. The debate was not whether he was the greatest current player in the world, but was he now the best we had *ever* seen?

After he claimed the first of the two prestigious individual awards in 2004, in the southern town of Chapecó in the state of Santa Catarina, which neighbours Ronaldinho's home state of Rio Grande do Sul, a statue was built in his honour. Made of fibreglass and resin and standing seven metres tall, the monument depicted him in his famous Brazil colours, holding a football in the palm of his hand and sporting his trademark buck-toothed grin.

He was so lacklustre and lethargic during the 2006 tournament that he almost looked disinterested. Questions were raised about his commitment to the national side now he was so hero-worshipped in Catalonia.

Two days after Brazil's early elimination, Ronaldinho returned to his home in Barcelona and immediately held a party alongside team-mate Adriano. That same day, almost 6,000 miles away, the statue in Chapecó was destroyed. 'All that is left is twisted metal. The burnt-out metal skeleton of a statue,' a town spokesman said in a quote to the media.

There is little doubt the vandalism was carried out by angry supporters of the now former world champions, but surely adding to the disgruntlement of the offenders was the current state of their local club team: Associação Chapecoense de Futebol (ACF), simply known as Chapecoense, 'Chape' in short.

With a population of just over 200,000 people, Chapecó is regarded as a Brazilian agro-industrial capital, as its land is dominated by farms, slaughterhouses and meat-processing plants. Whilst hard working and ambitious, the majority of the locals are very much working class and certainly in the bottom 50 per cent of the Brazilian economic structure, which consequently means bordering on the poverty-stricken.

Situated 500 miles south-west of São Paulo in the state of Santa Catarina, Chapecó is also one of the rainiest cities in the country. The weather sways between unbearable heat and tropical downpours, with far more of the latter throughout the year.

In the year 2006, Chapecó was known firstly for its agriculture and secondly for its incessant rainfall. But little did the townspeople know, their small city was about to embark on a footballing journey that would forever be their legend.

ACF was founded in 1973 following the merger of two local clubs, Atlético Chapecoense and Independente, in a bid by the executives of the clubs to create a team capable of qualifying for the national competitions, rather than merely competing in the State Championship: the *Campeonato Catarinense*.

From its inception, local politicians and business leaders were invited to make up the board of directors of the club. From these positions, whilst expected to financially support the team, they could make sponsorship and advertising arrangements for their companies and also influence the success of the *Clube de Futebol*, which would have a direct impact on the economy of the city.

The 12,500-capacity stadium Arena Condá (originally named Estadio Indio Condá in honour of the indigenous history of the region) was built in anticipation of a long and successful period. The stadium was, and still is, aesthetically representative of its team and of its people. It gives the impression of hard work, of industry, of a tireless and timeless work ethic. The design couldn't be simpler, as four individual concrete structures surround the pitch to create the north, south, east and west stands. There is no seating. Between 20 and 30 large concrete steps create the rows of terracing and whether the patrons choose to sit or stand is their choice. They stand.

The vertical face of each step is painted green, to give the illusion from ground level that the whole stadium surrounding the pitch is a wall of coloured support for the team. The horizontal face, however, is left its natural, dusty grey concrete colour. This avoids the hassle and expense of regular repainting due to being continually stepped on.

On each stand, at six unevenly spaced intervals, a series of rubber yellow blocks are placed on each row to half the depth of each step. The concrete of these strips is then painted the matching yellow tone to create the official stairways needed to comply with safety regulations.

Aerially, the stadium is ugly. It appears a huge block of dry, dusty concrete with random yellow strips running through it. Stand-alone floodlights are erected at each of the spaces created at the corners. But it represents Chape: practicality and pragmatism over style.

The offices and changing rooms required for the day-to-day running of the *Clube de Futebol* were simply built into the structures that created the stands.

The Chapecó residents, particularly those that attend the Chapecoense matches, keep a stock of clear plastic raincoats, so suddenly can a torrent come along. The whole crowd at the Arena Condá covered in these plastic sheets is a common sight.

The new franchise found swift success, winning their first State Championship, the *Campeonato Catarinense*, in 1977. The following year, *O Verdão* (the Big Green, the nickname they were given due to their all-green kit) competed in *Série A* and avoided *rebaixamento*.

In the 1979 campaign however, they failed to win a single game in the premier national division and were subsequently demoted to *Série B*. The descent continued as once again the crisis-ridden club failed to win a league game and suffered another *rebaixamento* into the third tier of the *Brasileiro*. This had been the year Ronaldinho was born in the neighbouring city of Porto Alegre. When the vandals tore down and torched the statue built in honour of their former hero 25 years on, supporters of the Big Green still had not seen their local side claw their way back above *Série C* and Chape were sitting outside the *Brasileiro*, playing in the *Campeonato Catarinense*. The Arena Condá was generally host to hundreds rather than the thousands of spectators it had been designed for.

Chape had managed to add a second state championship in 1996, but only after being embroiled in what was becoming typical Chapecoense controversy.

After reaching the *Campeonato Catarinense* Final, they would compete against Joinville in the home and away, two-legged match for the title. There was already some historic rivalry between the two clubs: the Chape glory of 1977 was the only interruption of a decade of dominance for Joinville, who won the state championship nine out of ten years between 1976 and 1985 and were expected to win a tenth title against the unfancied Big Green.

Going into the final, Chapecoense's best player was veteran attacking midfielder João Carlos Maringá. Short and squat in stature, he was 33 years old with thinning black hair and a neck so thick, his head almost seemed to be sat directly on his shoulders. He was a local man and Chape supporter, but had forged his footballing career with other teams in southern Brazil, before finally joining ACF in his vintage years. His experience and passion had meant he had been instantly installed as the changing-room leader and had an influence throughout the club, such was his immense popularity.

Maringá's best friend since school was of a similar age, build and physical appearance to himself. They were alike in every way, both warm and friendly and respected in the Chapecó community. His name was Sandro Pallaoro. They were so close, they called each other *'irmão'* (brother).

Pallaoro was building his business as a fruit and vegetable farmer and retailer. Like most in the city, he was hard working, ambitious and industrious, but making a good living was hard. So Maringá, using his connections with the *Clube de Futebol*, struck a deal for his friend: he would supply fruit and vegetables free to the cash-strapped club, and in turn, he would get a free advertising board for his promising enterprise.

The first leg of the final would be held in the Arena Condá, giving Chape home advantage, which they used in gaining a 1–0 victory to take into the second leg at the Arena Joinville. Similarities in the tactics could be drawn to those of Parreira, that had seen the national team take home World Cup glory less than three years earlier.

A tense and eventful game took place the following week: as the clock wound down the score was 3–2 in favour of Joinville. Therefore, the tie was locked at three goals each, with Chape set to take the title by virtue of the fact they had scored more goals at the opposition's ground, the 'away goals' rule used as a tie break in this type of match.

With the supporters preparing to celebrate, Joinville had a corner kick. It was played in from the right foot of the kicker, swinging away from the goal. A Joinville player headed it goalwards, past Chape's substitute goalkeeper, who was playing following the earlier dismissal of the first-choice *goleiro*. However, a defender guarding the goal line palmed the ball away illegally, but only to the feet of a Joinville attacker who slid the ball into the back of the net. The linesman frantically waved his flag as the referee blew the final whistle.

The Joinville players celebrated glory as their supporters stormed onto the pitch to join them. Meanwhile, the Big Green players appealed to the referee that the goal should not have stood.

In an extremely rare occurrence in the sport, after speaking to his linesman in the changing room, the referee disallowed the goal after the match. The flag had been waved to let the referee know the ball had gone out of play immediately following the corner kick before swinging back into play. The whole scramble which resulted in the goal should never have happened.

News leaked out of this decision and in an unprecedented event, both sets of players and supporters simultaneously celebrated being *Campeonato Catarinense* champions.

Joinville refused to accept the decision and the matter was taken to the courts, where it was judged that a final, decisive, single match was required and would take place at the Arena Condá stadium, Chapecó.

The night before the crucial game, the Joinville players and staff were staying in a Chapecó hotel, where the referee of the upcoming match was also resting, as was the president of the Catarinense Federation of football, who had ordered the decisive match.

A group of young Chape supporters decided to hold a party right outside the hotel, creating as much noise as possible, even setting off fireworks in an attempt to disrupt the sleep of the opposition.

The Joinville president called foul play and ordered his team not to take the field. Unfortunately for them, both the referee and Federation president had had a restful night in the same hotel and so judged the game should go ahead.

An impasse was created and, once again, the matter was taken to the courts, who said another decisive match should be played, but Chapecoense officials appealed, saying some of their players had now been allowed to go and represent other teams in the national tournaments, which take place in the second half of the calendar year.

Finally, on 18 December, six months after the initial game, the decisive match was held, in which Chapecoense still needed extra time before winning 2–0 and were finally awarded the 1996 *Campeonato Catarinense*, becoming state champion for the second time.

Chapecoense and their downtrodden supporters would go on to become even more grateful for the decision, as future glory was going to prove hard to find for a long time.

Around the turn of the millennium and for the years that followed, Chape competed in the wilderness of the state championships, as qualification for the national leagues got further and further out of reach.

Behind the scenes, the club was in an even worse predicament. They were in large amounts of debt and the facilities were poor. Players' welfare, nutrition and training was of extremely low quality, which was having a direct effect on the team performances. On occasion, players and staff had failed to be paid, resulting in many of them leaving. Court cases were set up as many individuals attempted to recoup what they were owed. The club had a reputation for being run like an amateur social club and as the debt grew, so did the strong possibility of bankruptcy and the liquidation of the club.

Late in 2005, a meeting was arranged at the corporate Hotel Bertaso by Chapecó Mayor João Rodrigues. He invited Chapecoense officials as well as local businessmen and entrepreneurs to discuss the future of the failing *Clube de Futebol*. When he finally got the attention of his generally disgruntled audience, he told them he saw two options: either issue the club with bankruptcy and winding-up orders, or spearhead a movement to give the people of the city an Associação Chapecoense de Futebol to be proud of.

Negotiations were long and arduous. The existing Chape directors were tired of the financial burden of the club and were looking to invest less time and money, not more. Some of the others, including the now very successful fruit and vegetable retailer Sandro Pallaoro, had had previous and unsuccessful business dealings with the club, and so were understandably sceptical.

On paper, this was not a good investment and Mayor Rodrigues had to be determined as he slowly won around his assembly and sold them his vision. He was aided by 60-year-old Plínio David de Nes Filho, a local business owner whose association with Chapecoense stretched all the way back to the club's 1973 foundation. He had held various roles on the board of directors and had invested his money religiously for decades, despite little or no success in return. He had repeatedly been asked to be the club president, but always insisted someone else was more suited to the role. Around the club, he was known as 'O Conciliador' (the Conciliator). In the background, his silent influence both financially and politically had been keeping Chapecoense in existence for decades.

The charming trio of Mayor Rodrigues, de Nes Filho and current Chape President Edir Félix de Marco began to draw conversation and intrigue from their previously withdrawn audience. There were suggestions of liquidating the failing club and replacing it with a new team, whilst some were pushing for a complete new name and branding for the club. But new President de Marco refused solidly.

Eventually a deal was made, enough funding gained and a new board of directors appointed, including Sandro Pallaoro, and the club was successfully restructured. Associação Chapecoense de Futebol remained in existence.

The facilities had reached such a state of disrepair that the Catarinense Federation had ordered improvements to be made followed by safety and fire inspections to meet the minimum requirements, or they may be expelled from the 2006 state championships or relegated to the second division. The newly structured board of directors acted swiftly and spent the funds required to meet the standards set by the Federation.

On the pitch, the only target was to not drop into the second tier of the state championships, which would spell oblivion for the football club. Two teams would be relegated, and after the scheduled ten rounds of matches, Chape were placed in the penultimate position. Luckily, the bottom four teams had been ordered to play a quadrangular series of matches to decide which teams would face the dreaded demotion.

The new board of directors fired the coach and frantically searched for someone to get the team in shape to perform better in the play-off matches. It was chaos as coaches came in for a matter of days whilst the search continued. Eventually, they approached Guilherme Macuglia, who was already in a post with another club, to lead the team for the short series of matches in a bid to save them. The experienced and well-travelled *técnico* came in and immediately brought in six players who he knew he could rely on from working with them in the past, picking them up on free transfers and loan deals. They included 32-year-old veteran goalkeeper Jose Nivaldo Martins Constante, known simply as Nivaldo.

The new coach and players had the impact required and Chape scraped second place in the mini-series and were saved, but only just.

The cup competition *Copa Santa Catarina* provides a secondary chance of glory within the region. The bigger and more established clubs who compete in the national leagues later in the year don't compete in this as the strain on their players is just too much. Miraculously, the Big Green managed to win the trophy, despite being in fundamental disarray.

Next on the agenda for the new investors was to rebuild the team for the 2007 campaign, beginning with a new head coach. The man they targeted as the new *técnico* was a former Chapecoense employee and current coach of Toledo, Agenor Piccinin. Ironically, he was one of the ex-staff members embroiled in a court case against ACF. President de Marco approached him and, despite the fact he harboured a grudge against the previous regime, Piccinin was charmed by the professionalism of the new directors, who promised him the salary he desired plus monthly instalments to repay what the club had previously owed him, instead of pursuing the court case. He accepted the offer and went to work constructing a team.

The positive movements of the club were being carried out in the public eye, and the community was abuzz at the thought of an exciting team to represent them for the first time in a decade.

The state championships regularly change format as the multitude of debt-stricken clubs rise and fall, liquidate or merge. The 2007 *Campeonato Catarinense* saw 12 teams compete in a league format, each playing the other home and away. After the 22 rounds of matches, the teams placed in the top two positions would play a two-legged match to decide who took the coveted championship.

The new manager and the experienced players brought in, particularly Nivaldo, used some of the additional funding and their knowledge to improve the training patterns, tactics, techniques and nutrition. They also insisted on using some of the money on hotel rooms for the evening before away matches, some of which were many miles away. This was to ensure the team were well rested and fresh for the game, rather than playing immediately after a long coach ride.

With the infrastructure further improved and the team getting stronger, with the confidence of the 2006 survival and *Copa Santa Catarina* glory, the momentum continued as the Big Green excelled themselves and finished second in the league format, setting up a grand finale against Criciúma, who had won *Série C* in the previous campaign and would be competing in the lofty *Série B* following the conclusion of the state championship. Already nine-time *Campeonato Catarinense* champions, Criciúma were expected to make it ten titles against the over-achieving minnows of Chape.

Just as in the final 11 years earlier against Joinville, the first leg was at the Arena Condá, and once again the result was the same. Chape managed to remain rigid and organised against the more skilled individual talents they were up against as they won the match 1–0. Once again *Era Parreira* tactics could be seen, in what was becoming the trademark style of Chapecoense.

Having stopped their rivals from scoring a vital 'away goal', Chape knew they had given themselves a chance of glory going into the second match in Criciúma.

But just 15 minutes into that match, the home side took the lead and were once again expected to go on to a comfortable victory.

However, early in the second half, the patient and disciplined Chape sprung a counter-attack and scored the precious goal that meant their opposition now needed to score twice to prevent a shock result. The *Série C* champions laid siege to the Chape goal, and eventually managed one of the two goals they needed to force a nervous final 25 minutes. The pressure continued and Criciúma committed more and more men forward. With ten minutes to go in the tie, the Big Green sprung another swift attack and scored, to complete the upset.

Once again, with their defensive *Parreira* tactics, Associação Chapecoense de Futebol had overcome the odds and were now three-time *Campeonato Catarinense* champions, just one year after facing both financial and sporting oblivion. This secured immediate qualification for the upcoming national *Brasileiro Série C*.

5

Flecha Verde

As *Série D* did not exist at this point, Chape's success in the *Campeonato Catarinense* meant a return to *Série C* in 2007, for the first time in almost a decade. It took the format of the current *Série D*, beginning with regional mini-leagues containing four teams each. The top two teams would go on to the knockout stages with dreams of making it to *Série B*, the bottom two returned to the obscurity of the state championships for 2008.

Chape won just one of their six games, but they had given their long-suffering fans a taste of the national game once again as well as their third *Campeonato Catarinense*.

On the pitch, the 2008 campaign was more inconsistent and they finished sixth in the 12-team state championship after dealing with multiple managerial changes and disruptions.

But their 2007 *Campeonato Catarinense* glory meant they had qualified for the 2008 *Copa do Brasil* for the first time, as the national knockout competition had only debuted in 1989.

In the first round Chape were drawn against successful *Série C* outfit Guarani FC. Due to the whole tournament being drawn out before the competition, both teams knew this match had a major prize: a second-round match-up against the mighty Internacional, who had won their State Championship, the *Campeonato Gaúcho*, almost 40 times. They had been *Série A* champions three times and in 2006 had won the top South American international competition, the *Copa Libertadores,* and even doubled it up with victory in the FIFA World Club Cup.

In typical fashion, despite their struggles in the *Catarinense* league, the Big Green caused an upset by beating Guarani 3–1 to advance and face Internacional, who were based in Porto Alegre, capital city of the neighbouring state of Rio Grande do Sul.

Off the field, Mayor João Rodrigues and club President Edir Félix de Marco continued to work at expanding Associação Chapecoense de Futebol. They pushed through permission to extend the stands of the Arena Condá to make it over 20,000 capacity. They gained government funding to drill and build an artesian well to improve the water supply to the stadium. They made a deal with the electricity company in which the new sponsors would share the bill, which was a major overhead cost for the stadium. As a result, profits from renting out the Arena for other games and events increased in abundance.

Improvements were made to the club restaurant and when some of the building extension work was done on the stadium, the supportive mayor rented some of it out as government office space, creating another source of income. Politically, Mayor Rodrigues was getting criticised for the time and financial assistance he was giving the *Clube de Futebol,* but public, health and education services were never neglected and he knew a thriving ACF would be invaluable for the community and the local economy.

In the weeks preceding the *Copa do Brasil* second-round match against Internacional, a game which would be played in front of a near-capacity crowd at the Arena Condá and televised to millions across the country, President de Marco contacted his counterpart from the major club. He was well respected in the footballing underworld of southern Brazil, having had a three-decade-long association with Chapecoense and was in his third spell as president: a stressful position which had to be juggled alongside the running of his own businesses. A large and charming man nearing 60 years old, he managed to strike a deal with the Internacional boss, who agreed to Chape taking 60 per cent of the total game revenue, including the national TV contract money.

The Big Green performed well against world-class opposition, losing the game 2–0, but raising almost $200,000. For a *Clube de*

Futebol not even in the national leagues, this would be enough to subsidise the remainder of the current campaign and the whole of the 2009 season, allowing all the small new revenue streams in place to be spent on improving the team. The extraordinary deal struck was the final great act of Edir Félix de Marco as his third and final presidential term came to an end.

Failure to qualify for any of the national competitions in the second half of the 2008 campaign meant extra time preparing for 2009. Changes were made at the club from top to bottom. Three of the local businessmen who had helped rescue the club and had become board members; Nei Maidana, Sandro Pallaoro and Jandir Bordignon, took on much more active roles as club president, vice-president and chairman respectively. A new coaching team was put in place and almost a complete new, small but talented 14-man squad was assembled with the minimum expectation of performing well enough in the *Campeonato Catarinense* to qualify for the newly incepted *Série D*.

One of the existing players retained was the ageing but still strong *goleiro* Nivaldo. Standing over six feet tall with short black hair and chiselled chin, he is physically imposing but also strong in character and had become popular and influential at the club, assisting the businessmen with the pure football issues. He insisted on the signing of a former team-mate who had become available, experienced 28-year-old defensive midfielder Cadu Gaúcho.

Cadu was, aesthetically, a very normal-looking human being, with pale skin and short, fair, thinning hair. He was of average height and did not possess a particularly athletic physique. He was, however, a leader of men. Well respected in the lower echelons of the Brazilian game, he was known for his great football brain, game management and on-pitch organisation. He orchestrated the team in which he played.

Other important newcomers to the club were Odair Souza, a 26-year-old midfielder commonly known as '*Neném*', and 25-year-old prolific striker Bruno Cazarine. Both brought experience of the lower levels of the *Brasileiro* and there were expectations of another successful *Campeonato Catarinense* campaign, especially amongst the loyal local supporters.

Here, I feel the need to address the Brazilian naming culture and how it integrates into their football.

Generally, the full name of a Brazilian male will be of multiple words in length, made up of given names, family names and regional and tribal titles. One or two or a derivation of these names will create the name the individual will be known as at a young age, but as the years progress, this name can change and evolve as nicknames are applied at various stages of life.

'*Neném*', which translates as an affectionate term for 'Baby', was a nickname given to Odair Souza due to his youthful appearance and small stature. Despite this being purely a nickname, it stuck so solidly it simply became his name. It appeared on the back of his shirt, on any medals he won and in any newspaper articles in which he appeared.

The full name of the other newcomer, Cadu Gaúcho, is Eduardo Luiz Preuss.

The most famous son of the country, Pelé, is actually Edson Arantes do Nascimento. His father was pro-footballer João Ramos do Nascimento, known as Dondinho, who first nicknamed his infant son '*Dico*'. A former team-mate of Dondinho was Vasco de Gama *goleiro* Bilé. Young Dico longed to be a goalkeeper and his hero was Bilé. He would mimic him on the field and shout out the name of his idol, but he had a slight speech impediment which made what he was calling out sound like '*Pelé*'. Pelé went on to be one of the world's most famous men from the whole 20th century, but hardly anyone across the world knows who Edson Arantes do Nascimento is.

The new presidential team of Maidana and Pallaoro brought in initiatives to try and make the *Clube de Futebol* the centre and most prominent part of the city. They visited schools to groom the future generations of supporters. They offered deals on the green and white replica outfits and on tickets for those coming to the games wearing the colours of the Big Green.

The 2009 *Campeonato Catarinense* took the format of a ten-team league, four of which would qualify for a second-round mini-league. The top two from this would both then qualify for the brand new *Série D* in the second half of the year and also go on to battle it out in the state championship final.

halfway point of the initial league stage, Chape found ...es just outside of the top four positions they needed. ..ongside them, also on just 13 points from the opening nine matches, were old rivals Avaí, who also had a strong outfit and were expected to be in a higher position.

Following the slow start, the new players of Chape settled into a rhythm with each other and were much improved, winning six of the next nine games to climb up the table. Avaí, however, won seven in the same period to finish the league on top, just two points ahead of Chape in second place. They were joined in the quadrangular semi-final by Criciúma and Joinville.

The good form of Avaí and Chape continued and after the four teams had played each other home and away, both had 11 points, but Avaí finished ahead due to one extra goal scored. Joinville had ten points; therefore Chape had qualified for not only the *Catarinense* final, but also for *Série D* by virtue of just one point.

The crucial players making up the backbone of the team had been veteran *goleiro* Nivaldo, strong defensive midfielder Cadu Gaúcho, diminutive playmaker Neném and prolific *atacante* Bruno Cazarine, who was the top striker in the competition after scoring a very impressive 17 goals.

Chape would host the first leg of the final, searching for their fourth *Campeonato Catarinense*, or their version of a 'Tetracampeonato'.

Almost 8,000 fans were in the Arena Condá as home advantage and the support of the ever re-growing and vociferous crowd got the Big Green off to a strong start and they went in at half-time one goal in the lead. Shortly into the second period though, Avaí scored a crucial away goal. Unless Chape could score again, they would face a huge task in the second match. Not only did they score, but they did so twice towards the end of the game and would take a 3–1 advantage to Avaí.

One week later, Chape looked set to comfortably win another state title as they cancelled out the Avaí away goal in the opening ten minutes and went a clear three goals ahead in the tie. This was the 26th match of the championship for the two teams in just a 15-week period, a huge demand on the small 14-man squad that Chape had just recently assembled. The fatigue began to show and Avaí applied the pressure, getting two goals and reducing the deficit to one at half-time.

The Big Green had to defend solidly for 45 minutes to take home the trophy. The tension mounted as the minutes went by, and with ten still to go, the pressure told and Avaí scored their precious tie equaliser. With the away goals rule in place, the only circumstance that could lead to extra time would be an exact reversal of the scoreline from the first leg, and that was the scenario as the match ended and an additional 30 minutes of play were ordered on the already physically broken Chape players.

Avaí scored three more goals in the additional time to take their 14th *Campeonato Catarinense*. There would be no '*Tetracampeonato*' for Chape, but there would be national *Brasileiro* football in the second part of the 2009 calendar, in the form of the first ever *Série D*.

Because football cannot be promised in the latter part of the year, players are only signed on short-term contracts. The deal for Neném was quickly extended. The strong performance in the championship of Cadu Gaúcho had seen him nominated for the state championship Player of the Season title at the awards evening in the state capital, Florianópolis.

He travelled to the event with his friend and chairman Jandir Bordignon. A quiet and thoughtful man, Cadu seemed solemn and distracted during the journey, and certainly not buoyed by the occasion. When Jandir asked him what was wrong, Cadu opened up about what his future held.

Gaúcho, fighting emotion, found the courage to break the news to Jandir that his fine form had led to an approach by *Série B* club América, and he had agreed to transfer to them, and would not be joining Chape on their adventure into *Série D*. The flight ticket had already been purchased by his proposed new team.

Bordignon implored him to reconsider, telling him how important he was to the Big Green; he attempted to sell his *amigo* the ambitions the board had for the future of the club. Cadu admitted he wanted to stay, but the extra money and prestige of *Série B* football was too alluring. He was 29 years old, and this may be his final opportunity to play in the truly big leagues of the *Brasileiro*.

Cadu picked up the award.

On return to Chapecó, Jandir Bordignon told the two people he thought could possibly appeal to the heart of Gaúcho the news, in the hope they could get him to stay. They were President Maidana and Cadu's old friend Nivaldo. They tugged at his big, heavy heart. They knew he felt the love of the club, of the city and of the supporters. He was told he would be the club *capitão*, and the team would be built around his influence.

Eventually, after consultation with his wife, he cancelled his agreement with América and stayed with Chape. He challenged himself to make it not just to *Série B* but above that level too, and to do so with the club he had fallen in love with: Chapecoense.

In the debut campaign of *Série D*, 40 clubs would compete in ten regional mini-leagues of four teams each. The top two teams from these would qualify for a five-round, two-legged knockout tournament. The four semi-finalists would go onto the new version of *Série C* for 2010. Following the restructure, the third tier of the hierarchy was a 20-team regional competition split into four leagues of five, that provided the security of the fact only the bottom team would be relegated back to *Série D*.

The remaining 36 teams of the 2009 *Série D* would go all the way back to competing solely in their respective state championships in 2010. The stakes of the *rebaixamento* system had never been so high.

Chape were grouped with *Série D* qualifiers from their neighbouring southern states. They were Londrina, of Paraná State, Ypiranga from Rio Grande do Sul and Mato Grosso do Sul's Naviraiense, a club only founded three years earlier.

It seemed a favourable draw for the squad, which was refreshed following a two-month break after their collapse in the state finale against Avaí. And so it proved. The Big Green comfortably won the mini-league, which gave them a favourable draw in the first knockout stage against a team which had qualified as a runner-up in their respective group. That team was Corinthians Paranaense of Paraná State, who had qualified from a weak group by just one point. Chape made the relatively short trip to the first away leg in the city of Curitiba and brushed the opposition aside 3–0 and comfortably saw the tie out in the return match in Chapecó to advance to the third round of the inaugural *Série D.*

A reunion with group stage opposition Londrina would provide more neighbouring action for Chape, who would go into this latest tie as favourites. It was less comfortable, but advance to the quarter-finals they did with an aggregate score of 3–2.

The quarter-final would be the most important tie in the recent history of Associação Chapecoense de Futebol. Victory would see them qualify for the final four of *Série D,* which would in turn confirm promotion to *Série C,* which under the new structure was no longer the bottom of the national *Brasileiro* and would therefore provide the Big Green the security that they would probably have national football for the foreseeable future.

The new *Série C* would be the highest level of football Chape and their supporters had seen in 30 years and would bring a new level of prestige and income to the club and the players, who were still on the poverty-imposing wages the bottom of the hierarchy provides. All this would mean they could offer the better players and new signings longer contracts and therefore give the club stability, something it had never had. Losing the tie and failing to go through to the semi-finals would mean dropping out of *Série D* and only having a guarantee of state championship football once again.

The quarter-final opposition would no longer be from a neighbouring state. In fact, they were Araguaia from the state of Mato Grosso, almost 2,000 kilometres from Chapecó. The city of Alto Araguaia is remote and surrounded by the Amazon rainforest. The bus journey would take more than 30 hours.

In 2006, the new board of businessmen had worked on the financial outgoings of the club. Previously, an external company had been used for all the travel arrangements of the team. To cut this expense, the board sanctioned the purchase of a team bus, but with a strict budget – after all, nothing special was required to transport the players and staff around the local clubs of Santa Catarina in the state championships. So, for less than $6,000, the club had bought a 1982 Mercedes Benz 1313 bus and emblazoned it with the ACF crest and green and white team colours. It was nicknamed *'Flecha Verde'* (Green Arrow). The opening match of the quarter-final tie would not only be the most important in the football team's recent history, it would be the biggest challenge in the 37-year existence of the bus.

Unsure just how long the epic journey would take, the team boarded *Flecha Verde* several days before the match and headed north. They finally arrived in Alto Araguaia two days before the big game, wanting nothing more than to disembark the decrepit old coach for the foreseeable future. To their horror, they discovered there were no hotels in or around the remote city, and they would have to drive a further 100km to the city of Mineiros to find accommodation.

It was a day of infernal heat when the match finally arrived, and *Flecha Verde* and the team had to make the two-hour journey back to Araguaia. Many days after the start of the trip, the team got to the destination of the football ground, and found a small, dilapidated stadium with a capacity of just 3,000.

The Chape delegation were shown to their changing room. Leading his weary troops was Chairman Jandir Bordignon, who immediately noticed a wasps' nest in the corner of the tiny, dirty locker room. Not wanting any further harm to come to his already dishevelled squad, he told them to wait outside whilst he took care of the venomous insects. He took a newspaper, rolled it up and lit one end to create the equivalent of an ancient explorer's torch and held it up to the nest, assuming the petrified inhabitants would flee out of the door and continue out of the building. Instead, they became incensed and attacked the charismatic chairman, who himself was the one to flee the situation, slamming the changing room door behind him, trapping the infuriated wasps inside. The flustered Bordignon shuffled back to his patient team and ashamedly explained to them they would have to get changed and prepare for the biggest match of their careers out on the street. The comical showing worked to lift the previously depleted spirits of the squad.

Despite the worst possible build-up to the match, Chape had the better players and managed victory in a tight game, by two goals to one. This meant going into the second leg, with Araguaia having the epic journey to overcome; the Big Green would have home advantage, a one-goal lead plus the added comfort of two away goals.

In celebration, the team decided to break up the arduous road journey home by crossing the border into Paraguay and visiting the city of Salto del Guariá, mainly to go shopping for electronics and lavish gifts for their partners, spending their winning bonus and what was sure to be a rise in salary for the all-but-secured promotion to *Série C*.

A week later, and in typical fashion, the torrential rain Chapecó seemingly saves for important game days came crashing down before and during the match. In the opening moments of the game, overzealous Big Green midfielder Fabrício committed a dangerous two-footed sliding tackle and gave the referee no option but to brandish a red card. Suddenly, the positive result which seemed inevitable was beginning to look questionable. There was some relief as 15 minutes in an Araguaia player committed a similar crime which was met with an identical punishment to bring the game to ten men versus ten. That relief was short-lived though as the unfancied opposition scored a goal to make it 2–2 on aggregate, cutting Chape's advantage to merely an away goal.

The rain saturated the field and turned the game into a circus. With every step of a player or bounce of a ball, a torrent of water would splash into the air. Visibility was almost non-existent and the ball simply could not travel along the ground.

During the second half, the rain turned to hail and the referee was finally forced to take the teams from the field and wait for a break in the clouds. Because of the huge sacrifice made by the travelling team to be there for the match, postponement was not a feasible option. The tension was agonising for all involved, with the stakes so high. Another goal past Nivaldo and Chape would be back to square one; hold on to the result and they would be in their highest position in the *Brasileiro* for 30 years.

When play resumed, every launch of the ball into the Chape penalty area led to a melee of sliding bodies, splashing rainwater and hearts in the mouths of the thousands of Big Green supporters. The anxiety level in the Arena Condá was palpable and all eyes were on the referee as he raised his whistle to his mouth and blew to signify glory for Chape. By the narrowest margin the rules of the sport offer – the 'away goal' – they had made it to the new, more prestigious *Série C* for the 2010 campaign, as well as proceeding to the *Série D* semi-finals.

In the final four, Chape would play Rio de Janeiro-based Macaé. The first leg would be played in the legendary and fabled Maracanã stadium: the national stadium and one of the most historic homes of football worldwide. The game was scheduled there rather than the small home of Macaé to whet the appetites of an 82,000-strong crowd for the sizzling match-up between Fluminense and Flamengo. The *Fla-Flu* Rio rivalry is one of the fiercest in the whole of world football.

It would be another fantastic experience for the Chape players, many of whom were still earning salaries that left them in poverty-stricken conditions.

Chape lost their semi-final to Macaé by four goals to three on aggregate, but the main objective had been accomplished and the city was now hooked on their over-achieving heroes.

Retaining the services of Cadu Gaúcho had proved invaluable. Neném, however, had picked up injuries and subsequently lost his place in the team.

Técnico Mauro Ovelha and the board of directors assembled a team they hoped would be capable of success at this new, higher standard. Some players left, many new faces arrived.

The 2010 campaign, as always, would begin with the latest edition of the *Campeonato Catarinense,* which would provide a good platform to gel the new team together.

After the first few rounds of play, many of the recent acquisitions weren't proving themselves worthy and were causing divisions with the old faces. Results were not good. The only brilliantly consistent performer was their leader and *capitão* Cadu Gaúcho, who was dragging his lacklustre peers through the tough period.

Gaúcho, however, was keeping secret the fact that after every spectacular match he played, he was experiencing excruciating pain in his hip.

After round eight of the championship, a brilliant performance in which Chapecoense lost 4–3 away at *Série B* favourites Figueirense and were finally feeling they were capable of competing with the big teams of the *Brasileiro,* the pain Cadu was going through became unbearable and he had to seek help. He had previously hesitated to do so because, deep down, he knew it was possible that something was seriously wrong.

The medical scans and diagnosis proved his concerns to be true: he had ground his cartilage in the area down to nothing and was constantly rubbing bone on bone whilst on the pitch. He was given a range of possible outcomes, including masking the pain to enable him to continue to play and also undergoing surgery. Both of these options were served to him with the warning that lasting damage and possible disability in later life were very plausible outcomes. The third option, though, was even harder to hear: that, at 29 years old and enjoying his football with Chape more than at any other time in his career, he hang up his boots forever.

Cadu held emotional discussions with his wife, Ana. They had a young daughter to consider and his long-term health was paramount. But football was all he knew, and his best way to provide a living for his family.

He talked to representatives from the club: President Nei Maidana; Vice-President Sandro Pallaoro; Chairman Jandir Bordignon; *Conciliador* de Nes Filho.

After two days of deliberation, he made the heartbreaking decision to walk away from the sport he loved to protect his well-being. He would not be joining Chape on their *Série C* adventures.

The club directors though, were quick to remember the loyalty Cadu had shown when he had been given the opportunity of the comparative riches of *Série B* less than a year beforehand, but had opted to stay with Chape. They knew that even if he couldn't take the pitch, his experience, knowledge and leadership skills could be utilised. They offered Cadu Gaúcho the role of director of football. His close relationship with the board combined with the high level of respect he had among the players meant he was perfect to act as a middle man between the boardroom and the changing room. His duties would include player welfare, scouting and transfers. Of course, he accepted the offer with eternal gratitude, and vowed to be as dedicated in his new role as he was in his previous one.

The form and fitness of Neném failed to fully recover to its highest levels and it was decided he would be loaned out to rivals Joinville for their *Série D* campaign, where he would have to prove himself all over again if he was going to be recalled to the Big Green.

With striker Bruno Cazarine long having left the club, Cadu Gaúcho a non-playing member of the staff and Neném out on loan, only the now 35-year-old Nivaldo remained of the team's backbone that had led the club to its recent successes.

Chape crashed out of the 2010 *Campeonato Catarinense* early and would have a long break from football before their eagerly awaited *Série C* campaign as the *Brasileiro* took its four-yearly break for the latest edition of the World Cup.

6

O Eterno

The low mood and lack of optimism of the Chape supporters and media during the summer of 2010 was shared nationally with regards to the *Canarinhos* adding a sixth *Copa do Mundo*, 'Hexacampeonato', in the impending tournament, held in South Africa.

The disconnection between the public and the national team had continued to widen. Not enough change had taken place following the 2006 disaster. Dunga, captain and leader of Parreira's 1994 winners, had been named successor to his mentor as the new coach. He symbolised *Era Parreira* and the style under him would continue to be uninspiring to the supporters who craved the return of *O Jogo Bonito*.

Another similarity to the previous squad was the exact same number of players who competed in front of their adoring fans domestically; once again only three of the 23-man squad were based in Brazil. The lack of money throughout the *Brasileiro* was being exploited by emerging countries with more wealth as clubs from the likes of Russia, Ukraine, China and Qatar even plucked the best youngsters from the Brazilian academies, offering their poverty-stricken families the kind of riches they could only dream of to take their children away in the hope they would come across the next Brazilian superstar. This was resulting in fewer talented, local, home-grown players coming through the *Brasileiro* system, adding to the disgruntlement of the passionate and obsessive supporters.

Veteran flair players Ronaldo, Ronaldinho and Adriano were omitted from the squad as Dunga went for younger, less skilled but more functional and conventional warriors to suit his style of play and work ethic.

The final and ultimate similarities with 2006 though came on the pitch, as the team again disappointed and again were eliminated at the quarter-final stage.

'THE END (DEFINITELY) OF THE ERA OF DUNGA: BRASIL...SAY A MELANCHOLIC GOODBYE TO THE *HEXA* DREAM' read the *O Globo* headline the following morning. It would be another long four-year wait for the nation, but at least 2014 would bring home advantage as Brazil were to host the tournament for the first time since 1950. Surely the festival fever would pull the nation back together to deliver the elusive sixth *Copa do Mundo* title?

Over three months had passed since the last competitive match of Associação Chapecoense de Futebol when they finally kicked off their eagerly awaited *Série C* campaign.

In an extraordinarily tight opening stage mini-league of five teams, despite spending most of the period in the bottom position which would have meant immediate demotion back to *Série D*, Chape found some much-needed good results late in the competition to save themselves and retain their third-tier *Brasileiro* status. It had been a tumultuous season: one that had taken its toll on the hierarchy of the club. Both President Nei Maidana and coach Mauro Ovelha had quit mid-season, with Ovelha later returning to his post.

The local press had been surprisingly scathing towards the club despite the heroics performed throughout 2009 to get to this lofty level, and the pressure had told on president and *técnico*. Expectations had been raised in the recent years of progress and because Chapecó is a city with only one *Clube de Futebol*, the local press coverage was comprehensive and sometimes intrusive, much like the national press treatment of the *Canarinhos*.

But the positive end to the season had lifted morale, as had encouraging news from Joinville, where Neném had enjoyed a successful return to form and fitness. He had helped Chape's rivals join them in *Série C*, but Odair *'Neném'* Souza would be back in the Big Green colours for the 2011 campaign.

With the leadership of the club still in question, no one from the board was keen to take on the responsibility of succeeding Nei Maidana as president, having seen the reaction of the press to a poor period, despite all his good work.

João Carlos Maringá was still a legend at the club. A great creative midfielder, he had been a key player in the late 1990s, including the controversial *Campeonato Catarinense* triumph of 1996. Since retiring as a player, Maringá had held many backroom positions at the club, and was immensely popular with the supporters and influential inside the club.

Before the start of the 2011 season, Maringá, a short but powerful-looking man with a thick, almost non-existent neck, went to see his childhood best friend, current board member and fruit and vegetable supply entrepreneur Sandro Pallaoro, at his farm.

Maringá implored Sandro to take on the presidency, assuring him he was the only man to take the club forward. Sandro resisted and resisted, but Maringá was determined and persuasive. Pallaoro decided to turn the tables on his friend, and told him he would accept the role of club president – but only if Maringá became his vice-president! The two negotiated their positions until two o'clock in the morning before eventually shaking hands on the agreement: Sandro Pallaoro and João Carlos Maringá would be club president and vice-president respectively going forward.

The two worked with director of football Cadu Gaúcho and managed to reinstate coach Mauro Ovelha in a hugely popular new management team that began to make additions to the squad.

Jandir Bordignon moved to a more commercial role and another local businessman, Mauro Luis Stumpf came in as finance director. The movements of the club once again seemed very positive.

As the beginning of the 2011 *Campeonato Catarinense* approached, Nivaldo, who would turn 37 years old during the competition, suffered an injury to his knee ligaments. The realisation that the talismanic goalkeeper was coming towards the end of his career dawned on the new football management team, who decided to bring in a new 'Number One'.

In a clear sign of the way Chape were now being viewed within the *Brasileiro,* they managed to bring in Rodolpho, a *goleiro* in his prime years at 29, who had spent the previous two campaigns playing in *Série B* for América. Nivaldo, when fit, would take on the role of reserve goalkeeper and mentor.

The forward momentum of the club successfully transferred itself onto the field as the Big Green, now regularly playing in front of several thousand supporters, imposed themselves on the ten-team league, coming out on top and looking set to complete a fourth state championship victory as they found themselves in a two-legged final against Criciúma. On this occasion, the rules dictated that in the event of a tie, the team who finished higher in the league stage would take the title, meaning Chape held the advantage. In the first game they went down 1–0 in Criciúma, which meant that in the return leg a week later in the Arena Condá, a victory for Chape would be championship glory. Any other result would mean failure.

Neném was still proving his form and fitness and had been a substitute for most of the competition, as he was again in the final. With less than 30 minutes to play and the scoreline still goalless, Criciúma were getting close to their tenth *Campeonato Catarinense* title. This was the time Mauro Ovelha decided to make an attacking change and introduce the creativity of Neném. Within minutes the substitute delivered the ball perfectly towards the goalmouth and the desperate Criciúma defender Carlinhos Santos launched himself towards the dangerous delivery and turned it into his own goal. It was 1–1 on aggregate and once again the Big Green held the advantage.

The scoreline stayed the same and Chape took their fourth championship in front of 15,000 delirious supporters. It was their own *Pentacampeonato.* The returning Neném had been the hero.

Under the previous rules, the game would have been locked even on away goals and the jeopardy of extra time and penalties would have been required. The Big Green had once again scraped over the line by the narrowest of narrow margins.

The momentum continued into the *Série C* campaign as Chape finished top of their initial group and qualified for the final eight, split into two regional groups. A top-two finish in the four-team mini-league would, staggeringly, result in the Big Green competing in *Série B* in 2012.

But the small, tightly knit squad put together by Cadu Gaúcho and his team once again fatigued and couldn't keep up the form, finishing third in the group, missing out by just one league place.

Chape were now looking up the *Brasileiro* with ambition and optimism rather than down with trepidation and fear. But at the conclusion of the 2011 season, coach Mauro Ovelha left the club in favour of rivals Avaí, hugely disrupting the plans the management team were making for the 2012 season.

Once again, led by Cadu Gaúcho, players and coaches were added to the squad. Cadu was particularly proud to add strong 25-year-old defender Rafael Lima to the ranks. Lima had served his apprenticeship with Figueirense and made himself a key member of their first team. His performances earned him a lucrative move to United Arab Emirates club Al Sharjah, where he had played for 18 months before coming back to Brazil.

Cadu also made a call to 31-year-old Anderson Paixão, a fitness coach who had served many *Brasileiro* teams including the likes of Grêmio following a brief spell with Chape in 2008. He was gaining a reputation for improving the strength and well-being of players; both mentally and physically.

Ten days after receiving the call from the popular and respected Gaúcho, Paixão arrived in Chapecó. Being a similar age to the players he would be working with, he was welcomed into the changing room and, with his broad smile and energetic personality, became one of the team.

With the new objective of making *Série B*, something which, just a few years previously, they could only have dreamt of, Chape could use the *Campeonato Catarinense* as a secondary competition in which the coaches could rotate the players to help keep the fitness of the small squad at its optimum for the main *Brasileiro* competition the club had now established itself in.

Therefore, Nivaldo returned as the main *goleiro* for the state championship, in which Chape struggled to find their best form, but with a new coaching structure in place and many reserve team players in the team, this was not unexpected. The Big Green failed to qualify for the *Campeonato Catarinense* final, but hopes were high ahead of the impending *Série C* campaign.

Rodolpho returned to keep goal as Nivaldo once again resumed his role as veteran understudy as the expectant crowds filled the ever-expanding Arena Condá for the opening games of the *Brasileiro*. But Chape made a slow start. The top-four finish which was required to qualify for the quarter-finals looked optimistic at best.

Following the poor start, changes were made to the team, including the return to goalkeeping duties of 38-year-old Nivaldo, who the supporters now nicknamed '*O Eterno*' (the Eternal).

Over the next six games, Chape gained 11 points to rise up the league, with Nivaldo conceding only two goals. But after a 1–0 defeat to bottom side Vila Nova, it was decided deeper changes would be made as Cadu Gaúcho and the management team attempted to bring in the personnel required. Although Chape were synonymous with the *Era Parreira*-style defensive tactics, what they were lacking was an *atacante* capable of reliably scoring the scrappy goals needed to win tight games. In the opening 11 games they had scored a pathetic total of only eight goals, but admirably only conceded the same amount.

Fair-haired Rodrigo Gral was, first and foremost, a fanatical supporter of Associação Chapecoense de Futebol, with the city being his hometown. A child prodigy, he was signed to the academy of super-club Internacional in the early '90s but signed his first professional contract with their arch-rivals Grêmio and went on to a career playing in *Série A* and *Série B* with various clubs. He represented Brazil at the 1999 FIFA World Youth Championships. Standing just 5ft 9in tall but with rapid pace, he was a predator of the penalty box and a terrific goalscorer. In 2002, at the age of just 25, he was signed by Japanese club Júbilo Iwata and, over the next ten years, went on to play for several clubs across Asia and the Middle East. But at 32 years old and with his beloved Chape now a club with enough standing to provide him the salary he deserved, Gral came to an agreement with Cadu Gaúcho to return home and finally pull on the Big Green shirt to provide the goals they so desperately needed. Not only would he add goals, but also experience and a passion for the club.

Also brought in was a new *técnico* Gilmar Dal Pozzo, who was known by connections of the management team and came highly recommended, even though he was not yet experienced as a *Brasileiro* head coach. The appointment was a gamble by Cadu, President Pallaoro and Vice-President Maringá. Tall, slender and shaven-headed, Dal Pozzo was a deep-thinking and intense coach who, it was hoped, would give the attacking players more confidence in front of goal.

Following the new arrivals, there were seven matches left of the scheduled 18, and Chape were sat in the middle of the standings. The 'Eternal' Nivaldo and his defenders continued to be infallible, conceding just four goals in those seven games. But the changes worked as the team plundered a spectacular 16 goals, with Gral amongst the scorers, and Chape raced up the standings to successfully achieve the top-four finish they craved by virtue of just two points.

Similarly to their vital 2009 *Série D* quarter-final, the opponents Chape were drawn against three years later in the *Série C* equivalent were also from the northern state of Mato Grosso, which meant another hellish journey aboard *Flecha Verde*. This time though, the first leg would be at the Arena Condá, meaning the team of Luverdense would have to perform the challenging and draining journey first. Dal Pozzo saw this as an opportunity; if the Big Green could continue their high goalscoring form against a potentially beleaguered team, they may be able to give themselves an unassailable lead ahead of their own long journey and therefore confirm promotion to *Série B*.

On 1 November 2012, in front of over 6,000 supporters in the Arena Condá, the team containing Nivaldo, Rafael Lima, Neném and Rodrigo Gral defeated Luverdense 3–0. One week later, following the two-day journey north, they successfully navigated a defeat by just one goal, which meant a two-goal aggregate victory, progression to the *Série C* semi-finals and promotion to the second tier of the *Brasileiro* for the first time in over 30 years.

Chape went on to lose the semi-final which meant that, once again, they had achieved their goal by the most minimal of margins.

The people of the city partied all night in the town square, it was a moment they thought they would never see: the Big Green in a non-regional, truly national 20-team division. They were officially one of the top 40 teams in the *Brasileiro* just five years after being in the wilderness alongside thousands of clubs battling it out in the state championships, hoping to climb on the first rung of the ladder and constantly battling financial ruin. Now though, they were guaranteed 38 *Brasileiro* matches in the second half of the season following the *Campeonato Catarinense*.

Série B status brought with it money from television deals and larger audiences inside the stadium: the work on the Arena Condá was almost finished, bringing the capacity to over 20,000 at the perfect time.

The challenge going forward was to maintain that level. If the players and staff could do that, they could have the lucrative careers that would change their families' way of life.

President Pallaoro watched all the games at the Arena Condá alongside his wife Vanusa, from a position amongst the fans rather than in a closed off observation box. They were supporters and became part of the community.

Vanusa, a dark-haired and friendly lady, took the responsibility upon herself to make the players' wives, girlfriends, children and families feel welcome and integrated at the club. This had a long-term benefit to the players – particularly the ones who moved to the city from afar, as their partners and families were happy and content. Over time, the warm, family feel in and around the club became unique. All the ladies socialised together, as did the children, as did the players.

7

Bruno

The status attached to the club's *Série B* membership enabled businessmen Sandro Pallaoro, Mauro Stumpf and Jandir Bordignon, president, finance director and marketing director respectively, to negotiate a huge sponsorship deal with major Brazilian banking chain *Caixa*. The financial future of ACF was now secured.

Cadu Gaúcho had developed into a brilliant director of football and his player recruitment was a vital ingredient in the progression of the club. When the management team decided they needed to strengthen in a certain position, Cadu would find a player with the hunger and desire to succeed, rather than players who had already had the success and may lack the same motivation. He would find out about the person as well as the player, about their lifestyle and their commitment to their profession – or lack of, as the case may be. Only players with the correct attitude would be sought after, and this was evident in the dressing room as the team developed as friends both on and off the pitch. The team members' families were always welcome and part of the club.

When Cadu had found a player with the right football skill set and personal attributes to be a good addition to the team, he would 'sell' the club to them, mentioning the management team, the changing-room bond, the relationship with the supporters and the club's ambition. He invariably got his man.

The step up in standard to *Série B* was a big one so some players of a higher quality would need to be added. But quantity as well as quality was required as the more intense and longer schedule would mean up to an extra 20 matches to be played. It was a huge undertaking for the management team to provide *técnico* Dal Pozzo with the tools he needed to keep the club in the league.

The addition of Rodrigo Gral, then approaching his 36th birthday, had been such an important part of the strong ending to the 2012 season that the lack of cover for him was highlighted as an area of concern, so Cadu and his team set about finding a suitable attacking option. He had long admired journeyman professional Bruno Rangel Domingues. Rangel turned 31 years of age on 11 December 2012, that same month he signed for Associação Chapecoense de Futebol.

From the Campos dos Goytacazes district of Rio de Janeiro, early in his career he played solely in the state championship for local teams, but left his club following the 2006 *Campeonato Fluminense* to take a job as a banking assistant, ironically with *Caixa*. He had given up on his footballing dreams in a bid to earn more money for his young family. But later that year, *Série C* side Ananindeua took a gamble on Rangel and offered him a short-term contract just for that small campaign. The gamble worked as Rangel scored eight goals. It would be 2009 before he would once again play in the *Brasileiro* third tier when he represented Águia de Marabá, then again in 2010 for Paysandu and in 2011 for Chape's rivals Joinville. In four *Série C* campaigns with four different clubs, Rangel had plundered 26 goals in 48 matches. Joinville were promoted in 2011 but only let Rangel play two matches in *Série B* before deeming him surplus to requirements. He had subsequently spent the 2012 season in *Série D* with Metropolitano.

Cadu Gaúcho had seen Bruno Rangel first hand during the seasons Chape shared *Série C* with him, and now he knew the almost 6ft tall, powerful, black *atacante* had a point to prove in the *Brasileiro*, having been dumped from the second tier by the old rivals of Chape, Joinville.

As a 'Top 40' club, a strong challenge for the state championship was expected, and with a deeper and more talented squad, Chape continued their momentum with a strong start in the 2013 *Campeonato Catarinense.*

To both protect Gral and also to give Rangel the chance to settle at his new club, the general tactic adopted was that Gral would start the matches but midway through the second half Rangel would replace him. Following two Gral goals in just the second game of the competition, with the scoreline at 3–1 against title rivals Avaí, the substitution took place. Within two minutes of his introduction Bruno Rangel crashed the ball into the back of the net to confirm a vital victory and score his first goal in the Big Green shirt.

Gral went on to be the top goalscorer of the whole competition, and with '*O Eterno*' still guarding the goal, Neném adding the midfield creativity and the other new signings of Cadu settling into the team, Chape were looking unstoppable and went on to finish top of the league.

Chape won their semi-final, but came up agonisingly short in the final against the only *Série A* team in the competition, Criciúma.

In the changing room after the match, coach Dal Pozzo greeted his crestfallen heroes who had come so close. 'God may have taken that chance from us here today to give us something at the end of the year of greater merit,' he said. He reassured his players with the fact they had won the league stage despite the presence of three established *Série B* teams as well as the eventual winners from the premier division. He told them they were a strong team, very capable of competing strongly in *Série B.*

Talismanic striker Rodrigo Gral rocked the preparations for the eagerly awaited *Série B* opening when he confided in the management team that he had some personal problems, and required an indefinite time away from the club to attend to his private affairs. Former banking assistant Bruno Rangel was now the first-choice centre-forward.

With the opening game just two days away, Chape travelled to the city airport where they were scheduled to board a flight to São Paulo before another bus journey to the city of Varginha, where they would play against Boa Esporte. But the flight was cancelled due to bad weather conditions. The team were forced to get back on the bus and take the eight-hour overnight road trip to Curitiba airport, where they were now scheduled on a 5am flight to São Paulo. They eventually arrived in Varginha the evening before the match, following an energy-sapping 24-hour journey.

The 39-year-old *goleiro* Nivaldo led his weary troops out onto the field. Coach Dal Pozzo again got the team motivated and as the first half progressed the adrenaline came to the fore. After 32 minutes of play, Bruno Rangel found the back of the net for his first ever *Série B* goal and the Big Green instantly believed that they belonged at this level.

Two minutes after the start of the second half, Rangel turned provider as he assisted newly signed defender Alan Ruschel to double the Chape lead. Third and fourth goals were to follow as Chape ran riot, Rangel book-ending the rout by getting the final goal and his second of the match. Only one round of games had passed, but Associação Chapecoense de Futebol were sat at the top of the *Brasileiro Série B*.

Just a few days later, the Arena Condá was to host its first second-tier match as Chape entertained local rivals Oeste. The expectations of the supporters following the spectacular opener were tempered as the Big Green played out a 1–1 draw, but Bruno Rangel was becoming a hero to the fans as he once again got the goal.

Match three put Chape on the road to São Paulo once again, this time to play São Caetano. The game was uninspiring and the travelling supporters could be forgiven for believing the fantastic opening performance was going to be the exception rather than the norm as the match entered added time as a goalless tie. But moments before the referee was about to call time, Chape defender André Paulino bustled the ball into the goal to regain the momentum of the Big Green machine and top spot in the league.

Chape remained away from home for round four but this time they went only to the capital of their own state of Santa Catarina to play Figueirense. They were expected to be beaten by a team who had played the previous campaign in *Série A*, but yet again Chape overcame the odds, and yet again Bruno Rangel was on the scoresheet in a 2–0 victory. This win, away from home over a local rival who had *always* stood way above Chape in the *Brasileiro* standings, meant a great deal to the supporters, who were now feeling the excitement that something special was happening.

Suddenly, a home tie against the lesser fancied ABC from the northern state of Rio Grande do Norte looked simple. And so it proved, as the Big Green rolled them aside by five goals to one. Bruno scored yet another two goals as Chape began to pull clear at the summit of the league.

One of new hero Rangel's former teams, Paysandu, came to the Arena Condá for round six. Chape were now expected, and expecting themselves, to win such a match and maintain the momentum. Confidence was flowing through the team, especially Bruno as he tracked back to out-muscle a Paysandu defender and take possession of the ball before spreading it wide left to the consistently excellent full-back, Alan Ruschel. Ruschel collected the ball and skipped past an onrushing defender before floating it into the penalty box where meeting it was the head of the airborne Rangel. The ball crashed into the back of the net before the goalkeeper could react at all.

Chape continued their dominance but failed to add a second goal and 20 minutes into the second half were punished as Paysandu broke away and scored with their first shot on goal. Undeterred, Chape resumed pressuring the Paysandu goal and it didn't take long for Rangel to once again punish his former employers as he slotted home from close range to regain the lead for Chape. The celebration of Bruno, pointing and looking to the heavens as he thanked the God he had so much faith in before hugging his adoring team-mates, was becoming an all too familiar sight.

As the players and supporters assumed their *Série B* lead was about to be enhanced as the 90th minute came, so did a lapse in concentration. With just their second shot on target of the match, Paysandu scored an equalising goal which would surely take the win, and the momentum, from Chape.

But just one minute after conceding the sickening goal, the effervescent Big Green players were back on the attack. Marauding left-back Alan Ruschel took the ball down the wing before wrapping his glorious left foot around it to deliver it into the penalty area where, yet again, it was met by the head of the leaping Bruno Rangel, who gently glanced it beyond the goalkeeper into the far corner of the goal. The game was won. Rangel celebrated his hat-trick goal by hurdling the advertising boards and launching himself into the supporters who now worshipped him so. The staff and players in the dugout hugged each other so strongly they fell to the floor in unison, with *técnico* Gilmar Dal Pozzo the bottom of the pile.

A straightforward victory over ASA followed as Chape began to pull clear at the top of *Série B* and for the first time the players, staff, management and supporters began to dare to dream about finishing in the top four positions, which would yield *Série A* football.

Week eight took Chape to old rivals Joinville, the team that had judged Bruno Rangel as not good enough for *Série B* two years beforehand and released him from the club. Joinville had also had a strong start to the campaign and a victory over Chape would see them close in on the surprising league leaders and heap the pressure on the shoulders of the Big Green.

At the halfway stage of the match, it seemed that would be the inevitable conclusion as the home team celebrated a two-goal advantage, whilst in the away changing room, Gilmar Dal Pozzo attempted to convince the Chape stars their unbeaten start to the season was not over yet.

The second-half performance following the team talk of Dal Pozzo was unrecognisable from the lacklustre first period, but when just 25 minutes remained Chape still trailed 2–0. Rangel, desperate to continue his scintillating form against the team that had shunned him, had barely had a sight of goal. But all he needed was one chance, which abruptly appeared, and he customarily lashed it into the goal of his former employers. It was great personal redemption for Bruno, but it would only truly matter if Chape could leave the city and return home with a positive result.

With ten minutes remaining, the Big Green got the goal which meant their momentum would continue. They were still unbeaten. Their biggest rivals would be kept at bay. They would remain clear at the top of *Série B*.

The following two matches were both at the Arena Condá, and both were comfortable victories, over América Mineiro and Avaí. Chape had an amazing 26 points from a possible 30. Only just over one quarter of the campaign had passed, and yet it looked ominously certain that Chape were about to achieve the holy grail of competing in *Série A*.

On current form, the week 11 fixture against mid-table Ceará was nothing to worry about. However, this brought about the most epic of all journeys: over 2,000 miles to the north-eastern coastal state of Fortaleza.

A surprising defeat by three goals to one saw the end of the unblemished campaign for Chape and alerted all associated with the club that the glory they were now quietly expecting at the end of the season was still far away.

The team stayed in the north east as just four days later they were to play their second successive away match in the region, this time in the state of Pernambuco, against Sport Club do Recife.

Recife too were enjoying a good campaign and were hopeful of finishing in the magical top four places, having only been demoted from the top tier in the previous season. They were just five points behind leaders Chape going into the match between the two. The winner would gain momentum as the season approached the halfway point and optimism would be high. Defeat would be worrying as teams queued up to take the lofty positions, and a second loss in a matter of days for Chape would add credence to the commonly felt theory in the league that the small, unfancied team would eventually fall away and pave the way for the clubs traditionally vying for a place amongst the elite of *Série A*.

These high stakes were shown in the tense bodies of the players in a relatively eventless first half. Supporters and spectators suspected both teams may well be satisfied to play out the tied result which would protect their strong positions. But just two minutes after the restart, Chape let down their guard and the star player of Recife, Marcos Aurélio pounced to punish them.

The Big Green went on the attack in search of a crucial equalising goal. Chance after chance came and went, as did the minutes. Sensing the huge win was close, the 17,000 Recife supporters became frantic, taunting the members of the ACF board who were watching from seats amongst the baying crowd. As the 90th minute came, Cadu Gaúcho decided to take himself and the other board members down the steps, up the tunnel and into the away team changing room for their own safety, anticipating a wave of delirious Recife supporters stampeding over them to invade the pitch at the final whistle.

Within seconds of Cadu disappearing with his colleagues, during yet another Chape attack, the referee saw an infringement inside the Recife penalty area and bravely pointed to the penalty spot. The 17,000 were now aghast as the new Chape icon Bruno Rangel placed the ball on the spot and calmly stepped back. At the sound of the whistle, he casually jogged up to the ball and drilled it straight into the middle of the goal, trusting the goalkeeper would gamble and dive one way or the other, which he duly did.

The now all too familiar celebration of Rangel pointing both index fingers to the sky whilst whispering a prayer to the God he worshipped so, as his team-mates raced to embrace him, subsequently ensued. He then, as he had many times before, approached the TV camera filming him, kissed his wedding ring and made a love-heart sign into the lens, all as an adoring message to his wife, Girlene and his two small children, Bàrbara and Daniel, who were over 2,000 miles away.

Bruno had moved his family all over the country for a decade in representing various lowly clubs to scrape a living for them. Finally, at the age of 32, the sacrifices were coming to fruition as his exploits began to make national headlines.

The game got back underway with just a minute or so of added time to play. The ball was launched towards the Recife goal where a defender had the seemingly simple job of clearing it away. But under the pressure of victory potentially being turned into defeat, he nervously snatched at his kick and missed the ball. To compound his mistake, the ball fell at the feet of the ruthless Rangel, who clinically and confidently lifted it over the onrushing goalkeeper and into the goal. This type of finish was becoming his trademark and was undoubtedly inspired by his hero, Romario. Rangel had been a talented 12-year-old in Rio de Janeiro when Romario, also from Rio, became a god to the whole of Brazil by being the star player that won the World Cup that hot July day in Los Angeles.

Seconds later the referee blew his final whistle. The stadium was silent with disbelief as the Chape players and staff celebrated the most unlikely of victories.

The jubilant men in green got back to the changing room where Cadu Gaúcho, unaware of the dramatic ending, assumed his warriors had managed to squeeze out a draw, based on their joy. Rangel was too humble to take the glory, so allowed his team-mates to collectively give their football director the stunning news, to the delight of Gaúcho.

It felt like three victories all at once, as they had repelled one of their closest rivals, gained three points and avoided back-to-back defeats and the pressure that would have provided. This spurred them on and the next four games reaped a further ten points and Rangel continued to find the net almost every time he took to the field.

Week 17 took Chape on the road to Bragantino, a small club from São Paulo, where they would play in front of less than 900 supporters in a late evening match. With the game still goalless after 35 minutes, Chape suffered a catastrophic ten minutes which saw them fall a goal behind, midfielder Athos receive two yellow cards and be dismissed and most worrying of all, Bruno Rangel sustain an injury and have to withdraw during the half-time break.

There would be no comeback from the shell-shocked men in green, and a second defeat of the campaign was inflicted.

Just days later, whilst it was assumed it would happen at some time during the arduous campaign, the 39-year-old body of Nivaldo broke down at the worst possible time. He would join star players Bruno Rangel, Neném and Rodrigo Gral on the unfit-for-service list, whilst top-class performer Alan Ruschel was serving a lengthy suspension having being caught up in a doping violation. The small squad was finally looking completely threadbare.

Lacking talent so badly, Gilmar Dal Pozzo brought Neném and Gral back from exile earlier than expected and named them as substitutes for the home tie against Icasa. Rodolpho was brought back to keep goal and untested youngster Caion debuted in attack for Rangel.

Despite throwing both Neném and Gral into the fray in the second half, it wasn't enough to save the beleaguered squad from a defeat by two goals to one. A second successive loss, and the pack moved tight behind the leaders.

The 2013 edition of *Série B* brought a rare but desirable member to its ranks. The mighty Palmeiras are one of the most supported teams in South America with an estimated 13 million fans. They are also the most decorated club in Brazil, having won the *Brasileiro Série A* a record nine times. They had suffered a poor top-flight campaign in 2012, finishing 18th and subsequently found themselves in the rare position of having to regain their place in the premier division.

The 19th match brought the halfway point of the season and the last team the leaders Chape were to go up against was indeed Palmeiras, who were ominously in second place, with just a single point separating them.

Travelling away to the São Paulo-based giants, and with his squad dilapidated, Gilmar Dal Pozzo sent out a defensive team in hopes of strangling a goalless draw from the match and retaining top place at the mid-point of the season. It was real *Era Parreira* tactics, showing heart and determination. It worked. The Big Green halted their alarming losing streak against all the odds and remained a point clear of their intimidating rivals. More importantly, they were nine points clear of fifth-placed Recife in their ultimate target of *Série A* football for 2014.

Seeing the name of their small, local club above that of the all-conquering and mighty Palmeiras in the *Brasileiro* at the season's mid-point brought a pride to the whole town, and belief that a miracle was on the horizon.

Brasileiro Série B standings; 5 September 2013 (top six)

#	Team	GP	P
1	Chapecoense	19	40
2	Palmeiras	19	39
3	Paraná	19	36
4	Joinville	19	31
5	Sport Recife	19	31
6	Avaí	19	30

GP = Games Played
P = Points

8
Danilo

Exactly two weeks shy of his ninth birthday, Marcos Danilo Padilha watched in amazement on the family TV set in the southern city of Cianorte as Claudio Taffarel etched his name into Brazilian folklore in Los Angeles 1994.

The inspired youngster was taken into the academy of Cianorte Futebol Clube (then Cianorte Esporte Clube), in the state of Paraná, where he developed into a talented young *goleiro*, making his first team debut in 2004. He had grown up hearing the phrase: *'Vai que é sua, Danilo!'* from his young peers, but was yearning for it to be yelled by a commentator of the stature of Galvão Bueno.

Considered slightly too small to be a truly top-level goalkeeper at just a touch over 6ft tall, 'Danilo' went onto embody the typical journeyman professional footballer as he moved around various small clubs in the state.

In 2011, 26-year-old Danilo found himself playing for lowly Arapongas, where he met and got engaged to his girlfriend Letícia dos Anjos Gabriel and subsequently moved into her parents' house as they could not afford a place of their own on the wages he was earning from football. Despite this, Danilo, known for his friendliness, positivity and beaming smile, insisted he would one day reach *Série A*, and even play for the national team that had inspired his goalkeeping career.

He then moved to neighbouring Londrina; a traditionally bigger club but currently battling it out in the state championship of Paraná, every year the target being qualification for the upcoming *Série D* competition.

The 2013 *Campeonato Paranaense* took on the format of 12 teams in one league division, where the winner of the first 11 rounds of matches would qualify for the final and also for *Série D*, and they would be joined by the winners of the second round of 11 games.

Despite a consistent high level of performance from Londrina, in particular Danilo, they heartbreakingly finished second in both halves of the competition, missing out on a place in *Série D* and tragically rendering the 28-year-old goalkeeper and his team-mates unemployed for the second half of the year.

Meanwhile, 500 miles south of Londrina, Chape resumed their exhilarating *Série B* campaign with two wins and a defeat. Bruno Rangel had continued his scoring heroics and Rodolpho had remained in goal in place of the injured Nivaldo. Chape had finally surrendered top spot to Palmeiras, but remained in a strong position despite their depleted squad, which suffered the ultimate setback when Rangel picked up another minor injury which would rule him out of the upcoming home tie against Figueirense, who were on good form and quickly closing in on the top four positions themselves.

Fitness coach Anderson Paixão was now proving invaluable as he worked tirelessly to ensure *técnico* Dal Pozzo had the best team possible available to him on each match day.

It was week 23 of 38 and the threadbare squad was lifted by the long-awaited and much-needed return of two heroes. The 'Eternal' Nivaldo regained his position the moment he was fit enough to do so and fellow iconic veteran Rodrigo Gral finally returned to the starting line-up to provide cover for the unavailable Rangel.

A crowd of 8,000 supporters were in the floodlit Arena Condá as the sun set over the stands. Mid-way through the first half, Big Green midfielder Athos collected the ball down the right side of the pitch before launching a long diagonal pass towards Gral, who was deep in the opposition penalty area. The 36-year-old fan-favourite peeled away from his defensive foe as the ball swiftly bore down on him. Showing his experience, fantastic finesse and natural goalscoring instinct, he jumped and cleanly headed the ball back across the goal, allowing its momentum to generate enough power and arc to bend around the airborne *goleiro* and into the side of the net to put his beloved Chapecoense one goal ahead in the crucial tie.

The stadium erupted with emotional delight. Their hero from the previous season had been through well-documented tough personal times and most thought they would never see him celebrating a goal in the Big Green colours again. He put his head in his hands and struggled to hold back tears of joy as his team-mates rushed to mob him in front of the delirious fans. Finally, an emotional hug from his loyal and faithful coach, Dal Pozzo.

The glorious and memorable moment was the final positive note of the evening for the men in green and their nervous entourage. The match finished in a draw, with Figueirense getting the equalising goal in a second half in which the Chape squad appeared to tire once again.

Games 24 and 25 came within three days of each other at the end of September and sent the Chapecoense delegation on another epic tour to the north of the country, to play against ABC and Paysandu respectively.

There were welcome returns for Neném and Rangel to the starting line-up, but yet again the ageing body of Nivaldo had broken down and once more Rodolpho would come into the team. An overall stronger-looking Chape would expect to gain the victory over the relegation-battling ABC.

But the inconsistent performances would continue and the Big Green found themselves a goal behind after 25 minutes. As half-time approached, the situation worsened when Rodolpho became the latest player stricken. He was replaced by third-choice goalkeeper Juliano, who was untried, untested and untrusted at this level of the *Brasileiro*.

The match concluded in a 2–0 defeat, and concerns instantly turned towards Paysandu, another team near the bottom of the standings. The Rodolpho injury was a bad, long-term one, so Gilmar Dal Pozzo had no choice but to persevere with Juliano.

Another late evening match under floodlights saw the worst possible start for Chape as the inexperienced goalkeeper watched the ball fly past him twice inside the opening ten minutes and despite a consolation last-gasp goal from Rangel, it was another defeat and they would return to Catarina from the epic journey with the campaign reaching crisis point.

After a seven-day break before the next match, Nivaldo would once again be rushed back. But with no trustworthy replacement available for him, and his dilapidated anatomy, Cadu Gaúcho and João Carlos Maringá deployed their attentions to find him an able deputy.

Once again the characteristics they would look for would be a hunger to succeed, a professional attitude and a commitment from the player to improving his career. But, crucially, it would need to be a goalkeeper readily available, so they would have to turn their attentions to someone currently outside the top four tiers of the *Brasileiro*, someone who had performed well in the state championships but missed out on promotion to *Série D*. Their careful and analytical search took them to one man: Marcos Danilo Padilha.

On hearing the news that the *Série B* high-fliers wanted to recruit him, even on a very short-term loan deal as the third-choice *goleiro* behind Nivaldo and Rodolpho, Danilo burst into tears, dropped to his knees and gasped, 'Thank you, God.'

For the forlorn team, a home tie against bottom side ASA was exactly what was required to get the potentially unravelling campaign back on track. Bruno Rangel scored yet another two goals as Chape returned to winning ways with a comfortable four-goal victory.

Week 27 saw a sterner test arriving at the Arena Condá in the shape of old rivals, Joinville. As well as the four-decade-long rivalry, the subplots for the match would make for a riveting occasion: Joinville were one of the few teams that could still realistically gatecrash the top four and potentially ruin the Chape dream, and despite scoring two goals in the earlier tied encounter, the talismanic Rangel still needed to gain a victory and place higher in the league than his former employers, to complete his redemption.

For the first time, Marcos Danilo Padilha saw his name on the Chape squad list as he was named on the substitutes' bench as the deputy to Nivaldo. It was becoming more apparent the injury sustained by Rodolpho would see him miss most of the remainder of the campaign.

With Nivaldo, Neném and Rangel all in the starting line-up, a recent easy victory behind them and the goalkeeping crisis alleviated, the Big Green walked out onto the pitch with rejuvenated confidence.

It was again an evening match at the Arena Condá in front of over 7,000 nervous supporters. Victory here would mean top-flight football was within touching distance, defeat would see their enemies close the gap. The anxieties within the stadium appeared to transfer to the players in the first half as the opening 45 minutes passed without any major event.

But just two minutes after the restart, a lapse in the Chapecoense concentration saw Eduardo put Joinville ahead.

Chape were struggling to make any breakthrough and it began to look ominous for the team in their changed strip of luminous green, rather than the dark, dour shade of the normal strip. But, not for the first time, the officials gave Chape an assist when they awarded them a penalty with less than 20 minutes of play remaining. It was yet another defining moment for Bruno as he casually placed the ball on the spot. Unlike every other person inside the stadium, and even the city, he looked unmoved as he began to approach the ball. His jog quickly turned into a sprint as he gained the momentum he required to lash the ball as venomously as he could down the centre of the goal and past the despairing *goleiro*. One-one.

As the minutes ticked by, neither team would be too downbeat with the shared points. It would mean Chape remained very strongly placed to complete the promotion miracle and Joinville would stay in the hunt.

But one man would not be happy to finish his season of a lifetime without a victory over the club that had previously robbed him of his dream. In the 94th minute of play, the referee had the whistle poised ready to call time at the next break in the game. Big Green midfielder Athos slid a glorious pass between the Joinville defenders towards the feet of Bruno on the edge of the penalty area. Sensing danger, the goalkeeper came rushing out to smother player and ball, but without even looking goalwards, Rangel caressed the ball high into the air and far over the head of the advancing opponent. The goalkeeper stopped his dash forward and stood helplessly flat-footed as he craned his neck backwards to watch the ball, which dropped almost vertically under the crossbar and nestled into the netting. It was audacious. It was sublime. It was redemption. It was ample call for almighty celebration on the pitch, in Dal Pozzo's technical area and, most vociferously, in the stands of the stadium.

The following three games yielded five more points as Chape clawed their way towards mathematical certainty and the unthinkable achievement. However, the goals were drying up for their hero, Rangel. Sensing that this meant they could afford to concede even fewer goals, *técnico* Dal Pozzo deployed his troops even more defensively, knowing a series of draws would be sufficient to get his team over the line. In true mastery of the *Era Parreira* style of play, Chapecoense astonishingly played out four successive goalless draws and with four matches left to play, a further four points was all that was required to complete the impossible dream.

Week 35 saw Chape head east to Paraná. With little more than ten minutes left to go, it looked like a professional soccer record of five consecutive 0–0 draws would be set. That was until the ball fell to the one and only Bruno Rangel, who crashed it into the goal to confirm his status as a *Deus* with the club and its supporters. It was his first goal after a barren spell of seven matches. It was the historic goal that made it all but certain that ACF would play *Série A* football in the year 2014.

Any remaining doubt lasted only four days when Chape hosted Bragatino and achieved the final point required in a 1–1 draw. Proving his importance yet again, the goal predictably came from Rangel.

With two games left to go, the Big Green had achieved a dream that had not even been on the horizon a mere six months ago.

Despite the fact he hadn't stepped out onto the competitive field of play, Dal Pozzo and the management team had been hugely impressed by the attitude, personality and talent shown by Danilo since his arrival. The talismanic Nivaldo had been magnificent and hugely influential in the success of the campaign and had no doubt earned a rest, so Dal Pozzo rewarded Danilo with a starting berth in the away trip to Icasa, in the northern state of Ceará.

The young *goleiro* knew this was potentially a life-changing opportunity. His current circumstances were that in a matter of weeks he would be returning to his parent club of Londrina to prepare for yet another arduous state championship campaign, whilst living at the parental home of his fiancée.

Icasa were still chasing one of the final promotion places, and had home advantage against a team that had travelled 2,000 miles following a huge celebration and could be forgiven for a lapse in concentration and commitment. Aside from that, Chape had only managed to win one match of their previous seven outings. They were not a team in good form and had rather stumbled over the glory line.

Predictably, the goal tended by Danilo spent the whole 90 minutes under siege. A massive 20 attempts and eight corner kicks rained down on him but he succumbed only once as Chape pulled off an unlikely 2–1 victory, despite having half the number of goal attempts than their opponents. Danilo was awarded the Man of the Match title, but, unbeknown to him, he had also earned a much greater reward.

In a poetic ending to the historic campaign, the final match saw the Arena Condá play host to the incomparable Palmeiras, who had predictably romped to the *Série B* championship. The victory over Icasa, earned almost single-handedly by Danilo, had assured Chape of finishing in second place, ensuring the metaphoric curtain would fall over the top two teams in the division. It would give the loyal supporters an appetite for the type of opposition they would see their beloved team against week after week starting just a few months later.

On a hot sunny day in Chapecó, the celebratory atmosphere was enhanced further as the dream finale was completed when a Bruno Rangel penalty gave the Big Green a 1–0 victory and a belief they were now successfully competing amongst the elite.

Brasileiro Série B 2013 final standings (top six)

#	Team	GP	P
1	Palmeiras	38	79
2	Chapecoense	38	72
3	Sport Recife	38	63
4	Figueirense	38	60
5	Icasa	38	59
6	Joinville	38	59

GP = Games Played
P = Points

The management and coaching skills of Sandro Pallaoro, Cadu Gaúcho, João Carlos Maringá, Mauro Stumpf, Jandir Bordignon and Gilmar Dal Pozzo were given universal acclaim as the rise of Chapecoense made national headlines.

Internally, the fitness work of Anderson Paixão, to merely get the squad through the campaign, was held in the highest of regards.

The 'Eternal' Nivaldo, approaching 40 years of age, would become a top-flight *Brasileiro* player following an exceptional campaign in which he conceded just 21 goals in the 30 *Série B* matches he played.

Bruno Rangel, having been signed as reserve striker, was now etched in Chapecoense folklore, having plundered 31 goals in just 34 outings in the Big Green shirt. He had finished as the *Série B* top scorer by an amazing nine-goal margin.

Associação Chapecoense de Futebol would play *Série A* football in 2014, and they would take Marcos Danilo Padilha with them to compete with Nivaldo for the *goleiro* position. To his emotional delight, the management offered him a relatively lucrative one-year contract and he moved his fiancée Letícia to the city of Chapecó to set up their new home and life together there.

With their future finally looking positive and affluent, Letícia gave Danilo yet more life-changing and wonderful news: he was going to be a father for the first time.

9

Obrigado e Tchau

2014 was no ordinary year for the *Brasileiro*; it was a World Cup year. 2014 was no ordinary World Cup year; it was the first year since 1950 that Brazil would host their precious *Copa do Mundo*. They desperately wanted to win every World Cup and expected to win most, but this one was on home soil; they absolutely needed to win.

Even though the *Esporte* pages of the media were awash with the most eagerly awaited sporting event of the generation, the miraculous achievements of ACF had also managed to make big news, both at home and abroad. The exploits of Bruno Rangel in particular had made global headlines. So much so, Al-Arabi of the super-rich Qatari Stars League came calling for his services.

Having just turned 32 years old, he knew his window of opportunity to earn truly life-changing money from the sport for himself and his family was a small one. He had had many dreams for his career as a young man, including competing in *Série A*, representing his beloved nation, playing abroad, earning enough money to drag his family out of the Brazilian poverty cycle.

Al-Arabi offered him an initial six-month contract worth more than he could earn in the whole year at Chape. So it was with the heaviest of hearts, Bruno Rangel decided he had to say an emotional farewell to his loyal team-mates, supportive club staff and adoring supporters as he and his family headed east. The streets of the rainy city of Chapecó now flowed with tears as the crowds gathered at the stadium to pay homage to their hero; to say thank you and goodbye; to say *obrigado e tchau.*

Bruno was not the only member of the over-achieving team of 2013 to attract attention from the richer clubs. Another was the brilliant full-back Alan Ruschel, who had made such an impact at the start of the season before getting a long-term suspension, that he had alerted *Série A* giants Internacional, who subsequently made him an offer that, yet again, Chape could not compete with. So, after only six appearances for the Big Green, Ruschel – another Cadu Gaúcho discovery – also left for pastures new.

Having spent three years as the very able deputy to the evergreen Nivaldo, waiting patiently for the day to arrive when the body of the veteran would finally give up permanently, Rodolpho also moved on. Along with most at the club, he could see the talent of Danilo and knew there was finally a worthy challenger to the number one jersey that the Eternal one had held for so many years.

Despite being financially stable, especially compared to the crisis-years less than a decade before, Chape still could not compete with the *Série A* clubs in terms of facilities. Their budget was, by some margin, the lowest in the league and a tiny fraction of that of the established, traditionally bigger teams.

They were the only club in the division without their own dedicated training complex. Even after its extension and renovation work, the Arena Condá paled almost embarrassingly when compared to the stadia of most of the top-tier clubs.

Only after the promotion was the ancient team bus *Flecha Verde* finally made redundant.

Some of the fantastic and diligent board members including Mauro Stumpf and João Carlos Maringá had still been volunteers in their positions and had not taken a penny from the club in payment for their services. As a *Série A* club, the workload these individuals now had to achieve meant they finally became full-time employees of the *Clube de Futebol.*

So Stumpf, Maringá, Cadu Gaúcho and Dal Pozzo once again set about rebuilding the squad using free transfers and loanees. They targeted rejected players from the big, rich clubs and young, hungry and potentially talented players from the lower leagues they knew so well.

The general consensus within the *Brasileiro* and the media was that the fairy tale story of Chapecoense had reached its peak by them merely being a member of the illustrious premier league for one season, and surviving relegation would be an even bigger miracle than the series of promotions that had brought them there. Chape would surely just be masquerading as a team worthy of this lofty position, playing week in, week out, against squads chock-a-block with the kind of talent they could only dream of.

Finishing the campaign in 16th of the 20 teams and avoiding immediate *rebaixamento* would be regarded as an astonishing achievement.

The 2014 *Campeonato Catarinense* saw ten teams compete in a league format where they each played one another just once with the top four teams going on to qualify for the play-off.

Chape were one of only three *Série A* clubs in the competition and subsequently expected themselves to perform strongly and possibly achieve their '*Pentacampeonato*', their fifth state championship.

The Big Green would travel to one of the lowliest clubs in the competition, Juventus SC, a team who had been outside the national *Brasileiro* structure almost 20 years.

An almost identical team took to the field that had represented Chape in their rise through the lower ranks, including a goalkeeper swiftly approaching his 40th birthday and Rodrigo Gral, a striker taking back his place as the spearhead of the team, coming up to his 37th.

It was roles reversed for the players of Chapecoense, who had spent so many years rising up to their position of lowly underdogs in the top flight. But if they were to perform respectably in *Série A*, Juventus SC were a team they would expect to brush aside with ease.

In front of a crowd of less than 700, it was back to state championship reality for Chape as they suffered an embarrassing two-goal defeat.

In the second match of the championship they would face another lowly minnow in Marcílio Dias, but this time at the Arena Condá in front of almost 4,000 supporters. They would welcome back a familiar face; their former deputy goalkeeper Rodolpho was now representing Dias and was expecting a busy day keeping his former team-mates at bay.

But once again the veterans of Chape looked slow and tired and the few new faces weren't having the impact it was hoped in replacing the likes of Bruno Rangel and Alan Ruschel. The team looked disjointed and uninspired.

The Big Green stars ashamedly trudged off the pitch at half-time losing by one goal to nil.

In the second half, Chape managed to draw level, but required an own goal by the opposition to finally beat former charge Rodolpho. Frustrated Marcílio Dias player Serginho immediately picked up a second yellow card and was subsequently shown red. Chape were now on level terms, at home against a team from outside the *Brasileiro* who were minus one player. They had 30 minutes remaining to rescue the alarming situation. But Rodolpho repelled attack after attack.

With less than ten minutes to go, the unthinkable happened; a counter from Dias saw Nivaldo helpless to stop Chape falling behind once again.

It would be a mortifying result for all associated with the club. But just when his beloved team needed him, with just minutes remaining, Rodrigo Gral finally managed to squeeze the ball past his friend Rodolpho to spare the blushes of his team-mates. Unbeknown to everyone at the time, it would be his final goal for Chapecoense.

Despite a rise in the level of performance and results towards the end of the league phase of the state championship, Chape finished outside the four play-off places, with arch-rivals Joinville and *Série D's* Metropolitano amongst the teams to qualify at their expense. It was bewildering and worrisome form ahead of the upcoming *Série A* campaign, and changes were going to be needed.

Realising he could no longer perform to the high standards he had set during his illustrious career and not wanting to let his beloved Chapecoense and its supporters down, Rodrigo Gral had his friend João Carlos Maringá call the media to the Associação Chapecoense de Futebol press office, where he gave an emotional and tear-filled statement in which he spoke of his recent turmoil. He highlighted the love he had felt for the club since his childhood, before individually thanking President Sandro Pallaoro as well as the other directors who had allowed him to achieve his dreams of not only playing for Chapecoense, but leading them to glory.

Struggling to hold back his emotions, he thanked the whole Chapecó community for their faith and support, before going on to talk of the special energy in the changing room, naming *técnico* Dal Pozzo as well as leaders such as Neném and Nivaldo as being mainly responsible for the unique atmosphere. He had scored 24 goals in 51 matches for Chape and passed the landmark of 500 career goals there.

Finally, he spoke of his hopes for the team in *Série A* and his confidence about how they would perform, confirming he would be in the stadium, standing shoulder to shoulder with his fellow Big Green supporters, watching his 'warriors' continue to achieve greatness.

The Eternal Nivaldo had played every minute of the disappointing *Campeonato Catarinense* and his 40th birthday had passed in that time. Meanwhile, Danilo had continued to impress in training. The time had finally come for Nivaldo to step aside; Marcos Danilo Padilha was now the first-choice goalkeeper for a premier division *Clube de Futebol.*

The final change to the upcoming line-up would be an enforced one, as Neném sustained yet another injury that would keep him from his long-awaited debut at the top tier of the *Brasileiro*, after more than a decade playing in its lower echelons.

On 20 April 2014, *Série A* football finally returned to the city of Chapecó as Chapecoense hosted Coritiba at the Arena Condá.

Gilmar Dal Pozzo made changes to the team that had struggled so much with lesser opposition and once again sent out his troops with the defensive style akin with *Era Parreira*, hoping simply to stifle the game and achieve the minimum of a draw, one league point and to recover some confidence.

The mission was accomplished as Chape ground out a goalless draw, largely down to Danilo, who was still a complete unknown at this level. He made seven saves to achieve an unexpected point for his coach, his team-mates and his supporters.

A week later, the Big Green travelled to a familiar rival in Sport Recife, who had joined them in promotion from the second tier and would no doubt be one of the teams fighting alongside Chape for survival in the big league. Chapecoense lost 2–1.

Meanwhile, 12,000 kilometres away in Qatar, Bruno Rangel was approaching the end of his six-month lucrative contract and had made a decision regarding his future: no amount of money could make him as happy as playing in front of his adoring supporters at the Arena Condá.

'I'm coming back to the place where I was at my happiest, always treated well and in which I had the best time of my career. Now, I have to count down the days until I leave Qatar and help the team and Gilmar and make fans happy. They have given me so much strength over the past year,' Rangel said in a statement.

'To play abroad was a dream come true. It was very important for me and my family; having concluded that phase of my life, I am coming back to a place where I learned how to love. I want to give all that happiness to the community of Chapecó, and I want to be happy again in Chapecoense.'

To the delight of the supporters, Cadu Gaúcho had secured the return of the talismanic striker, but with time remaining on his Middle Eastern contract and the *Brasileiro* taking a ten-week summer break for the World Cup, it would be some months before the Chape faithful saw their hero in his Big Green shirt once again.

The first two weeks of May saw two of the *Brasileiro's* most historic and richest clubs come to Chapecó as the Arena Condá played host to Corinthians Paulista of São Paulo and Grêmio from neighbouring Porto Alegre. Almost 20,000 supporters squeezed into the stadium as the decade-long vision and investment of Mayor João Rodrigues, Sandro Pallaoro and the board of local businessmen and managers came to fruition.

Despite remaining solid and defensive, as instructed by coach Dal Pozzo, knowing they were up against clearly higher-level players, Chape narrowly lost both games by just one goal. The pressure was beginning to mount on Gilmar Dal Pozzo, along with doubts about his unproven ability at this level.

Série A status also brought with it automatic qualification for the *Copa do Brasil* and Chape would play host to Ceará of *Série B*. Despite taking an early lead, they succumbed to another defeat. Following the poor Catarinense campaign, the questionable start to *Série A* and now elimination from the cup competition, the pressure on Dal Pozzo was mounting. Head coach turnover in Brazil makes English football management seem secure!

Week five of the league campaign provided a better opportunity for Chape to gain their first *Série A* victory with an away trip to Paraná state to play fellow strugglers Atlético Paranaense. Neném was returning too but was only fit enough for a place on the substitutes' bench.

The starting team was almost unrecognisable from the Chape squad that had blazed its way through the *Brasileiro*.

A very late equalising goal to earn a 1–1 draw and a second *Série A* point was enough to save the job of Dal Pozzo, despite Chape now sitting bottom of the league.

A Catarina state derby was next as Chape visited local rivals Criciúma in round six. Chape fell behind early. Knowing another defeat could see him dismissed, Dal Pozzo put on Neném with 20 minutes to go. At that moment, Odair '*Neném*' Souza became the first player in Brazilian football history to play in all four divisions for the same club; but he was helpless to stop time running out and Chape falling to yet another narrow defeat.

Sandro Pallaoro, João Carlos Maringá, Cadu Gaúcho and the board met immediately after the match to discuss the crisis and ultimately make a decision on the future of the loyal *técnico*. Should they allow him the whole campaign in charge or make a change whilst the club still had time for a recovery?

The following morning, on Friday, 23 May 2014, President Sandro Pallaoro, after speaking to Dal Pozzo, called in the media for a press conference. The ACF media room at the Arena Condá was abuzz with nervous energy, but then fell silent at the announcement of the departure of the coach, describing it as a 'difficult but necessary' decision. The president went on to say it was difficult because Dal Pozzo was so popular with the leaders in the changing room and described him as 'the greatest coach in the club's history'. The return of Bruno Rangel had not come early enough for him to save the job of his friend.

Cadu Gaúcho gave a statement admitting that 'perhaps this will not be the best decision, but with the situation, change was necessary'.

The search began for a new permanent *técnico*. In the meantime, assistant coach Celso Rodrigues was promoted to interim head coach. The decision had to be made so swiftly as another mammoth match was just two days away; Palmeiras were once again heading to the Arena Condá. Dedicated and popular fitness coach Anderson Paixão would assist Rodrigues.

The duo were appointed to maintain some continuity and to appease some of the disgruntled veteran players. They had adored Dal Pozzo; in only two years he had taken them from mediocre lower league journeymen, struggling to provide a living for their families, to stars of *Série A* playing in front of tens of thousands of supporters and earning riches the type of which they had previously only dreamt.

Gilmar Dal Pozzo spoke of his time at the club with no bitterness on how it ended, in a later interview. 'I would love one day to work again at Chapecoense. Honestly, I don't know if it will ever happen. Anyway, I need to reiterate once again my gratitude for everything that has happened, to have written and been part of the club's history.'

Despite the difficulties on the field, it was still hard to find Danilo without a beaming smile upon his face. His personal performances were good and he was living out his wildest dreams. When he returned to his new home of an evening, he and Letícia barely spoke of *futebol*. They joyously discussed baby names and what sex they thought the child was going to be. She wanted a girl, but Danilo desperately wanted a boy who he could teach to play *O Jogo Bonito*.

For his first team selection, Celso Rodrigues was able to include the now fully fit captain Rafael Lima and playmaker Neném from the start. With Chape appearing to lack both leadership and goal-scoring creativity, this was very welcome as Palmeiras came to town.

The São Paulo giants had made a strong start to the campaign, but the Big Green had beaten them at the Arena Condá less than six months earlier, in the final match of their glorious *Série B* season. With that memory instilled in them from their new, albeit temporary *técnico*, and a stronger-starting 11 taking to the field than in recent weeks, the Chape stars confidently strode out onto the pitch.

But when the game got underway, it was Palmeiras in the ascendancy as they pressed forward and attacked the goal of Chape. However, they came up against an inspired Marcos Danilo Padilha, who was equal to all the opposition could throw at him. With just moments remaining until the half-time interval, which Chape had been hoping to reach with the tie goalless, they launched a counter-attack. The ball was diagonally switched to right-sided full-back Fabiano, who was marauding forward at full speed. He took the ball in his stride and slid it across the goalmouth into the path of striker Tiago Luis, who calmly passed the ball into the back of the net. The players mobbed the goalscorer in celebration; meanwhile, at the opposite end of the pitch, Danilo pounded his chest and the Chape emblem on his jersey and screamed towards the joyous crowd, who knew the lead was largely down to their *goleiro*.

The shell-shocked stars of Palmeiras failed to recover from the surprising scoreline during the break and came out performing like a shadow of the team they had looked during most of the first period. Just two minutes into the second half, a Palmeiras defender failed to clear the ball. It subsequently fell to Big Green midfielder Dedé, who beautifully curled the ball back around the body of the player at fault and beyond the unsighted goalkeeper into the bottom corner of the net.

There would be no way back for the crestfallen stars as Chape saw out the two-goal victory. Danilo was awarded the Man of the Match title having made eight saves and he was now a firm favourite of the supporters and was achieving his dreams. This was the day he came to the attention of the whole of the *Brasileiro* and cemented his future as a top-level *goleiro*. The one-year contract was certainly going to be enhanced and extended following a display like this. Even more importantly to him, this was also the day he became a father. He rushed to the side of Letícia straight after the match and welcomed his beloved baby boy Lorenzo into the world.

Six years after facing them as a lowly club sat outside the national leagues, Chape would once again go up against the mighty Internacional. The previous, historic *Copa do Brasil* meeting had been the event where then President Edir Félix de Marco had negotiated a deal to take the majority of the proceeds to halt their financial difficulties; a true turning point for Chape and one that helped initiate the momentous rise through the leagues.

Despite the clear rise in confidence levels from the Palmeiras victory, this was an extremely tough task as they made the short journey to the neighbouring state, Rio Grande do Sol. Internacional had made a strong start to their campaign, and on this occasion the form book would not be turned on its head by Chape, who found themselves on the wrong end of the 2–0 scoreline.

A familiar and welcoming face was on the substitutes' bench for Internacional in the form of Alan Ruschel, who embraced his friends and former team-mates.

Spirits remained high in the Chape camp. In Corinthians Paulista, Grêmio, Palmeiras and Internacional they had already challenged themselves against four of the biggest and best that *Série A* had to offer; they had managed to win one of these games, only conceded five goals and scored three. Despite being 18th out of 20 in the league, they were proving competitive at the highest level with their *Era Parreira*-style tactics and an inspired *goleiro*.

So, a home tie against comparatively smaller club Bahia was clearly a winnable encounter.

It was the first day of June, and just 11 days before the Brazilian national team opened the 2014 *Copa do Mundo* in São Paulo, when Chape hosted Bahia. Following this ninth round of matches, the *Brasileiro* would take a break of over two months to host the tournament dubbed 'the Greatest Show on Earth'. Victory would mean all associated with Chape could enjoy the World Cup in a position of strength, with their club outside the bottom four teams that made up the *rebaixamento* zone.

It took a world-class volley into the top corner to beat Danilo and give Chape a nervous final few minutes, but before that they had performed well and scored two goals, looking extremely comfortable. They won the game and celebrated at the final whistle as if it was the season's finale. By the time they resumed their dramatic journey, Bruno Rangel would have returned home.

In the happiest period of his life, Danilo could support his beloved *Canarinhos* alongside his wife and baby son, safe in the knowledge their future was one of joy and affluence.

Brasileiro Série A standings; June 2014 (bottom six)

#	Team	GP	P
15	Bahia	8	8
16	Chapecoense	9	8
17	Coritiba	9	7
18	Vitória	9	7
19	Flamengo	9	7
20	Figueirense	9	4

GP = Games Played
P = Points

10

Copa do Mundo: Fase de Grupos

Born just two months after Marcos Danilo Padilha, I too know what it was like to be an awe-inspired eight-year-old watching the *Copa do Mundo* 1994. I had already got the football bug, a hereditary condition passed down to me from my Dad. I spent the early nineties watching Alex Ferguson ready his Manchester United team for an all-conquering generation, and tuning into Channel 4 for their legendary coverage of Italian football.

In the summer of 1994, the bug developed into an incurable fever. What I saw then was passion on an unprecedented scale. Blood, sweat and tears of both joy and despair.

Watching Brazil lift the World Cup in the sweltering American heatwave, with the sunlight gleaming off their golden yellow shirts, the World Cup combined with Brazil almost seemed mythical in my mind. They had Samba-dancing players and colourful supporters. The fact it was my first international tournament as a football fan and England had failed to even qualify made it seem all the more elusive. I would eagerly await the next international tournament, and every two years from that point onwards, when it arrived, my life would be put on hold for the duration of it.

When I heard the 2014 tournament was going to be held in Brazil, I knew I had to be there.

Brazilian optimism for World Cup glory and the elusive *Hexacampeonato* this time around came from two sources: home advantage and 22-year-old genius Neymar Jr. The host nation invariably overachieved in every tournament as the wave of impassioned fanfare inspired their players, intimidated opposition and somehow managed to subconsciously influence the decisions of the match officials. Even more to the forefront of their minds than that, however, was the fact their heroes had not lost a competitive match on home soil for almost 40 years, when Peru shocked them in the 1975 *Copa América*.

In Neymar Jr. they had their latest superstar, a status confirmed by his financially mind-boggling move to the resident home of any current Brazilian talisman: FC Barcelona.

Looking beyond him, however, the *Canarinhos* squad looked weak. Four were domestic residents of the *Brasileiro*, but now the standard of player export to Europe had diminished. Historically they had been the top stars in England, Spain and Italy; now many played in secondary standard leagues such as Russia, Ukraine and France.

The 2002 World Cup winning *técnico* Luiz Filipe Scolari had returned to lead a far less talented generation than had been available for his previous period.

I couldn't have asked for a better pair of friends to be going on the trip of a lifetime with than the very differing brothers, Si and Jono.

Si is the older sibling. Pale and ginger with a receding hairline and blotchy complexion; he's very funny and always has a story to tell. He is a Leeds United supporter.

Jono has darker hair and skin. More measured and sensible, when compared to his brother at least. He is a Manchester United fan.

We would spend a total of six weeks in Brail, regardless of how our home nation faired. I'd booked us a three-bedroom apartment in the famous Ipanema district of Rio de Janeiro over a year in advance; before England had even qualified for the tournament.

As the World Cup grew closer, the media began scaremongering about Brazil; publishing crime rates and airing multiple documentaries on TV about the culture of drugs and violence in and around the *favelas*. Life appeared tragically cheap in these areas.

Our families began to worry; our friends became provocative – even organising a raffle over what day our first mugging would take place!

I was in regular text message contact with our landlady, Leila, about various arrangements. She didn't speak English and was clearly using a translating tool to send the messages as well as to interpret mine. She seemed amazing; so welcoming and eager to do as much for us as she possibly could. I asked her if she could assist us with getting hold of tickets for the World Cup matches. The ballot system put in place by FIFA heavily favoured the locals. It was generally accepted that many of the poor local Brazilians would get tickets and then be able to decide whether to attend the game and embrace the festival atmosphere that the tournament brings to a country just once for each generation; or whether to sell them on for a much-needed profit and benefit that way.

Leila put me in contact with a friend of hers, Sergio. He spoke fantastic English but after an ill-fated attempt at a telephone conversation, in which a combination of him speaking in his second language and my broad Yorkshire accent making me hard to understand, we too decided to stick to text messaging.

Sergio kindly offered to try to source some tickets and would sell them on to us at the same price he had paid, and would provide proof of his transaction, if we wired him the money.

I had succeeded in the official ballot to get tickets to England's final game of the group stage, the *fase de grupos*, against Costa Rica in Belo Horizonte, as well as a quarter-final match in the capital, Brasilia. We had booked and paid for flights and accommodation for these trips from our Rio base.

As a live sports and international football lover, I was also desperate to go to a match at the legendary Maracanã stadium in Rio. I had studied the tournament breakdown well enough to know that should England finish runner-up in their tough group, they would play their first knockout match there.

Sergio pointed me towards a social media page where local Brazilians were selling the tickets they had been lucky enough to be awarded in the ballot. I found and contacted a girl who had four tickets to that very match. She was called Lorraine and again, she seemed lovely. We agreed a reasonable price and she said she would hold onto them for us until we arrived in Rio and we could meet up and pay in cash.

Whilst the apartment was expensive to hire for that length of time, Leila could clearly have gotten a higher rate for it nearer to the start of the tournament; but she had told me she didn't believe in exploiting people the way virtually every other accommodation vendor in the country was.

She had also offered to have us picked up from the airport and brought to the apartment. We were due to land quite late in the evening on a Thursday, the opening night of the World Cup. The whole situation was beginning to seem too good to be true and our friends and family began to doubt the intentions of the people we were in contact with. The insinuation, given the perception created in the media of every Brazilian having criminal intent, was that we had left ourselves open to a potentially dangerous transaction and situation.

Could Sergio also be trying to exploit us by asking us to send him money for tickets? He was friends with Leila after all? Possibly even Lorraine had an ulterior motive?

As we walked into Arrivals at Rio's Galeao Airport, a huge beaming smile immediately caught my eye. It was Leila. She was holding up a sign with my name upon it and she welcomed all three of us with a hug. Accompanying her was a taxi driver friend of hers, who she had prearranged for the occasion.

It was Thursday and the opening night of the World Cup and Brazil, as hosts, were playing against Croatia following the lavish opening ceremony.

FIFA had set up free-to-enter fan parks at each of the hosting cities, with Rio's 'Fans Fest' on Copacabana being the epicentre of the whole event in the world's most football fanatical country. Brazil were in action in the opening match of the tournament as we made our cab journey. As a result of this, the city streets were eerily empty as we drove to the apartment. Leila instructed her friend to take advantage of the spacious roads and take us on a little sight-seeing tour on the way, including the iconic Maracanã stadium.

The final part of this adventurous journey was a drive along the Copacabana front, where we could see, hear and feel the raucous atmosphere emanating from the Fans Fest, which looked to us like a sea of light and colour with yellow shirts as far as the eyes could see, against the majestic backdrop of the South Atlantic Ocean horizon, over which any anxiety about what we were to expect on arrival had now disappeared.

We arrived at the apartment and Leila showed us around. I noticed Jono quickly and sneakily move his luggage into the biggest bedroom. There were two large rooms with double beds and flat screen TVs on the wall, and one tiny bedroom with just a single bed and no space left to fit anything else in it. There was no way after all the efforts I had made organising this that I was going to end up in what was effectively a linen cupboard. So I left Si communicating with Leila in broken English and a series of hand gestures whilst I put my bags in the other big room. Poor Si was to spend the five weeks in what was basically a tiny corridor between two toilets.

At the end of each of the three beds was a gift; pairs of locally made, high-quality flip-flops.

After we paid Leila, she and her friend left. We continued to explore the apartment; on opening the fridge, we saw a bucket full of ice containing six bottles of beer, as well as multiple containers full of homemade food Leila had prepared for us.

I couldn't have been happier as I felt redemption for the initial faith I had shown in Leila, but almost a little embarrassed I had briefly doubted her intentions. She is a truly lovely lady.

We unpacked and made ourselves at home. We drank the beer, ate the food and watched the remainder of the opening game of the tournament on the huge TV. Brazil duly won, but not without a scare, having fallen behind to Croatia. Talisman Neymar scored two goals to prove just how reliant his overbearingly expectant country were on his young shoulders. One of those goals was a penalty kick and Oscar added an injury-time third to put a gloss on the unconvincing performance.

We had plans for our first day: go for some food and get our bearings around our new neighbourhood, then head to Copacabana for the festival of football. The late evening match was a mouthwatering event: defending champions Spain up against the always entertaining and popular Netherlands.

Back in the 1994 American edition of the *Copa*, Brazil and the Dutch had played out the best match of the tournament at the quarter-final stage; the *Canarinhos* running out winners by three goals to two in an exhilarating encounter that helped forge my obsession. Both teams had subsequently become the nations I turned my support to once the inevitable had happened and England had been eliminated from any major tournament.

It was approximately ten minutes' walk from our Ipanema apartment to the corner where the two legendary beaches of Ipanema and Copacabana met, then around another 20 minutes the whole way along the Copacabana front to where the Fans Fest was situated.

A long 64 years had passed since the last World Cup finals tournament had seen the shores of this football frenzied nation, and anticipation was in the air as we walked along the beach front. Hundreds of TV and radio stations had set up camp along Copacabana and we were spotting famous ex-footballers and pundits from all over the globe.

The FIFA Fans Fest was an amazing event. A village of bars, giant screens, stalls, attractions and entertainment, all upon the golden sandy beach. One of the tournament sponsors was a Brazilian sun-cream manufacturer. They had representatives handing out a sachet of their product per visitor. When they got to us, they gave one to me, one to Jono and then said to Si: 'You can take as many as you want!' referring to his outrageously pale complexion.

Appearing on stage between the games there were DJs, bands and a guest appearance from the legendary Ronaldo. The *cerveja* (beer) flowed and anticipation grew.

That first day, as well as the Spain versus Holland match in the evening, Mexico and Chile were in action, and their fans were represented fantastically in Rio. It was unadulterated fun. Every person there had a smile on their face as they interacted with like-minded strangers from anywhere and everywhere.

The sun descended over the Copacabana horizon and darkness set in as the big game approached. The crowd was extremely partisan towards the ever-popular Dutch, who were huge underdogs for the match against the recently world-dominating Spanish. And it was the defending champions that took an early lead. They had become synonymous with low-scoring wins in which they dominated possession of the ball and this game appeared to be heading the same way as half-time approached, when Dutch defender Daley Blind punted the ball up field towards star striker Robin Van Persie. Spain goalkeeper Iker Casillas rushed from his goal line to intercept, but to everyone's amazement, 'RVP' attempted an almost impossible diving header from 20 yards out as the ball dropped from the sky over his left shoulder. The ball rebounded off his forehead, over the onrushing Casillas and into the top corner of the goal. I don't know how many thousands of people were on that beach that evening, but in the open-air environment it felt like the whole world had erupted into cheering.

The Dutch team themselves must've felt the surge of adrenaline, as they emerged for the second half and were completely irrepressible, running riot to beat the tournament favourites 5–1.

The day had been a truly amazing experience, everything I'd hoped for and more during the months of nervous anticipation. It only served to increase the excitement for the following day, when we would again be on Copacabana for the opening game of England against World Cup specialists Italy. But rather strangely, I wasn't too concerned about the result of the upcoming match. I was desperate for England to finish runner-up in the group which would confirm we would be seeing them play in the second round at the Maracanã. It was perceived to be a three-way competition for the two qualifying places, between England, Italy and Uruguay. Costa Rica were regarded as the group's 'whipping boys'; they were a tiny nation of less than five million people and minnows in the football world. So, if we beat Italy, we would probably go on to win the group.

Uruguay were thought of as somewhat of a one-man team in the shape of Luis Suarez, who was one of the world's best players and had excelled in the English Premier League the previous season with Liverpool. But, as a neutral supporter you had to passionately dislike the snarling, cheating genius who was getting repeatedly banned for violent acts against opponents.

England narrowly lost against Italy. I have watched my national team play in stadia the world over, but the atmosphere created that day overshadowed them all, and yet we were on a beach. A very memorable experience.

Costa Rica had sprung a shock by beating Uruguay.

The following morning, I was researching the ramifications of these results over my coffee when my studying led me to the realisation it was Sunday; this epiphany was coupled with the recollection that Sergio, despite failing to get any tickets for us, had requested our company for the afternoon. He wanted to meet us and show us around and could only do it on a Sunday afternoon due to his work and family commitments. I checked my text messages and, sure enough, the date had been made and we were to meet him at a shopping mall and he had prearranged a taxi to collect us from the apartment at noon. The traffic in Rio is notoriously terrible, and with the added thousands of people in the city for the tournament, it would have taken him all morning to come and collect us.

On the very stroke of midday, a car horn sounded from the street outside. Somewhat hungover, we dashed to the waiting cab. We all climbed into the tiny car, which had a multitude of dents, scratches and differing coloured panels. I climbed into the front passenger seat, my friends in the back.

Argentina were playing Bosnia in Rio that day, so the city streets were awash with the sky blue and white striped shirts of the Brazilians' arch-rivals.

We'd only travelled a few hundred metres to the corner of our street when our driver stopped the car at the side of a small group of Argentina-shirted supporters. He leaned over my lap and opened the glove compartment whilst casually whispering, 'Just allow me to get my weapons of mass destruction.' He grabbed a handful of something unidentifiable as I looked tentatively over my shoulder at Si and Jono, who were also wearing similar dubious expressions on their faces.

The driver's window wound down as he launched what turned out to be a handful of fire-crackers at the floor next to where the gang were stood, before immediately speeding off up the street with a screech of the tyres and black smoke. We spun our heads around to see the aftermath as all the panic-stricken white and blue-clad supporters were swiftly scattering in different directions, clearly fearing the gun violence synonymous with the surrounding *favelas* had struck them.

Meanwhile, the driver was casually winding up his window and readjusting his sunglasses whilst we were open mouthed and silent with shock, before we simultaneously began nervously laughing at what we had just witnessed.

We arrived at the mall car park, Sergio (clearly more adept with modern technology than myself despite being of the older generation) had sent his location to my mobile device. Sure enough, there stood a very Hispanic-looking middle-aged man with tanned skin, thick swept-back black hair and sunglasses that looked so natural they gave the impression that he had been born with them across his face.

He was leaning on the door of his car; a very old and small Fiat Panda. He greeted us warmly and his gentle manner instantly put us at ease. He insisted we follow him as he dashed through the mall and snuck into the service staircases. Up and up we went until we came out onto the flat roof, which gave the most mind-blowing view of the whole city, and he told us some stories and history of the specific *favelas* we were looking at and some of the extraordinary architecture.

He then drove us around the whole of Rio, describing in detail all of the sights and sounds. The horrendous traffic on this occasion proved to be a positive as it gave Sergio time to tell us what we were looking at and share more anecdotes about the surroundings.

He showed us the football stadia of Rio, including the ancient ground of the mighty Flamengo, which was surprisingly close to our apartment, and also that of his beloved Botafogo. This was where my interest in the trials and tribulations of the *Brasileiro* began.

We then visited his favourite seafood restaurant. It was off the beaten track, with not one tourist in sight. We enjoyed wonderful food and a great authentic reflection of Brazilian life.

Next, he then drove us along the scenic coastline to a small bar that overlooked a quaint, small section of beach. He ordered us all a *coco-agua,* which was a large coconut with a hole bored through it for a straw to access the natural water. Whilst this was amazingly refreshing, the three of us ordered a *cerveja* each too.

Sergio then drove us back to our Ipanema apartment, again taking the scenic route along the coastline. It created a majestic view, but suddenly he anchored on the brakes and performed an erratic U-turn on the busy main road. Fellow road users let their feelings be known with the sounding of horns and gesturing of hands.

He had seen the Bosnian team bus parked in a hotel car park and insisted on having his photo taken with it for his 'World Cup Album'.

The official FIFA team buses were loud and colourful; they couldn't be missed. And sure enough, once we were back on the road and travelling in the correct direction on it, Sergio spotted another one further up the road. It was Argentina! He sped up and began to weave between the cars, activating the sound of more horns as he tried to catch up to Lionel Messi and the rest of the Argentinian superstars. As our vehicle finally drove parallel to the bus, he insisted I take photos of him driving whilst he posed with the coach in the background of the picture, all this whilst travelling around 50 miles per hour on the highway.

Sergio is a crazy man, but the nicest crazy man I have ever had the fortune to meet. And I have met many.

Inspired by a Christmas gift of a Portuguese phrase book, during the long period of anticipation for the trip I had downloaded an audio book in an attempt to learn some key words and phrases I thought would be most useful. A couple of these were proving particularly useful: *trés cerveja por favor* (three beers please) and *onde estao os banheiros por favor?* (where are the toilets please?). After finding a barman who spoke no English, Si decided to attempt it himself: he proceeded to request *tres banheiros por favor* (three toilets please). The look of bewilderment on the bartender's face was something to behold.

Both the locals and supporters of the other nations were generally fantastic and wonderfully friendly. Some who had been there for the opening Brazil match advised us that the Fans Fest may not be the best option for the upcoming second game of the home nation.

Every *Canarinhos* match for the tournament had been declared a national holiday. Quite simply, every person in Brazil would be in front of a screen for the match, and as many as possible would attempt to be on Copacabana beach.

So as a venue for the imminent match, we were recommended 'The Jockey Club', a World Cup village set in Rio's majestic racecourse. At the southern point stood a giant screen with the Ipanema skyline as its backdrop; to the north, the mountainous landscape, including the awe-inspiring Christ the Redeemer, overlooked the venue. There were bars, shops, fairground rides, restaurants and nightclubs.

The atmosphere building there for the Brazil match was extraordinary. Live bands and DJs meant the party never stopped as the anticipation grew for the match. I sat and watched the army of yellow and green-clad individuals sweat and fidget with excitement for the upcoming match but with anxiety over the result. The release of this excitement and anxiety came during the live coverage of the national anthem, when the horde let their passion loose in a mesmerising display of unity.

But a lacklustre *Canarinhos* played out a dull draw with Mexico.

The day of the crucial England match against Suarez and his national team of relative journeymen was upon us. All the planning and expense would be instantly justified with a victory that would almost guarantee us seeing England play a World Cup knockout match at the fabled Maracanã. A draw would also be acceptable; meaning we would be travelling to Belo Horizonte for the Costa Rica match in a state of nervous optimism.

Uruguay were second only to Argentina in the league table of rivalry with Brazil, which meant there was a very partisan pro-England atmosphere in Rio. The animosity towards Uruguay went back to the last time Brazil had hosted the World Cup in 1950, when 200,000 crammed into the Maracanã to witness the *Canarinhos* win their first *Copa do Mundo* in the final against Uruguay and they led 1–0 at half-time. But Brazil went on to surrender the lead in the second half and slump to the first of the catastrophic, shattering defeats that caused such depression and painful memories which survived through the generations. That was their original footballing tragedy.

Ominously, for the first time since we arrived, a tropical storm hit the city about an hour before the scheduled kick-off time. Brazilian rain of that ilk is completely alien to what we have in the UK. It is a deluge. This was the type of incessant rain to which the residents of Chapecó have become accustomed on a very regular basis.

We, along with almost all the other England supporters on Copacabana, ran to a large British-themed pub close by that we had already frequented on a few occasions. The atmosphere was something to behold. The adversity created by the weather appeared to have galvanised optimism. Englishmen of a variety of ages and backgrounds were chatting, drinking and singing together. None that I spoke to had quite as much at stake on this result as we did, with tickets and travel expense for two matches on the line.

For me, time never passes so quickly as when I am transfixed and emotionally invested in a live sporting event. It seemed like the match had only just kicked off when Suarez – of course it had to be Suarez – gave Uruguay the lead with a header. In reality, it was almost half-time, which came and went in a flash as everyone charged for either more *cerveja* or the *banheiros*. We needed a goal in the second half.

I watched minute pile upon minute on the match clock possibly more than I was watching the game itself. England were playing well. Uruguay were under pressure and couldn't get the ball up field to talisman Suarez. The pent-up nervous energy grew and grew but was released into glorious celebration when Wayne Rooney tapped in a goal with 15 minutes to go. The cheer which erupted was deafening but short-lived as attention turned back to the screen: this game could now be won. England were looking like the team most capable of another goal. But failing that, the draw was acceptable and would keep our dreams alive.

Five minutes to go. Out of nowhere, a long ball from the Uruguay goalkeeper sailed over the England defensive line and Suarez, having barely touched the ball in the second half, was suddenly bearing down on goal. He clinically and powerfully dispatched it past *goleiro* Joe Hart.

Heartbreak.

England were out of the tournament. The trip to Belo Horizonte would be for a glorified friendly match. The Maracanã tickets we had agreed to buy from Lorraine would most definitely not be to see my beloved Three Lions.

Not only was the travel to Belo a disheartening ordeal, it also meant we had to miss the final group game of the *Canarinhos*, which was taking place concurrently with our flight north. I felt a sense of loss not being amongst the adrenaline and excitement of our now fellow Rio natives.

On landing in Belo, we discovered that Brazil had beaten Cameroon by four goals to one with Neymar once again scoring two of them. The result confirmed top place in their mini-league and a city-wide street party was taking place in Belo to celebrate this.

The following day we headed to the stadium, which was truly magnificent and it was a pleasure to be at the home of the current and all-conquering *Série A* champions: Cruzeiro.

The game, however, was a truly woeful goalless draw. However, as the effectively pointless game failed to offer any excitement to all the England fans who had clearly sacrificed so much to be there, we all collectively created our own entertainment in the form of ironic songs and Mexican waves. In the end, it was very memorable and enjoyable.

The joyous atmosphere was compounded by the Costa Rica supporters; the draw meant the underdogs of the group had finished as its winners and qualified for the knockout stages.

11

Copa do Mundo: Fase Eliminatória

Our return to Rio coincided with the end of the World Cup *fase de grupos* and beginning of the knockout stages: the *fase eliminatória*. This meant for the remaining three weeks of the trip there would be an average of one game per day, as opposed to the relentless three per day of the two weeks up to this point.

The relaxation of the football calendar was going to give us the chance to finally see some of the famous sights of Rio, such as excursions to Sugarloaf Mountain and to see Christ the Redeemer.

But first of all, we decided some time should be spent on the famous beach of Ipanema. We armed Jono's man-bag with the stereotypical things Englishmen need for a day at the beach: sunglasses, sun cream, a selection of screwed-up notes of local currency and, on this occasion, Si's digital camera. We strolled southwards through the blocks of shops and apartments until the ocean horizon came into view.

On stepping on to the golden beach, we realised we had stumbled on to the far eastern end of the two-mile-long stretch of sand. It was a particularly quiet area; we looked up to the west, where two mountains called the '*Dois Irmãos*' (Two Brothers) rise and provide a glorious backdrop to that end of the beach. In between was a vibrant array of colour and life. As we turned on our heels to head west, Si performed a double glance in the direction of a silver-haired gentleman laid stomach down on his towel, reading a book.

'That's Gary Lineker!' Si excitedly yelled. Sure enough, it was the legendary England striker turned TV presenter. Being a couple of years older than me, Si remembers Lineker score goal after goal in the Three Lions jersey and describes him as one of his heroes. 'Let's go get a picture with him!' he exclaimed.

'Ok,' was my response.

'Oh, do we have to?' Jono said with a sigh. He was concerned about the three of us embarrassing ourselves and disturbing the clearly relaxing star.

'Yeah, come on, get the camera out Jono!' was Si's defiant response to his sibling.

Whilst Jono delved into his man-bag, myself and Si approached Lineker, politely said hello and asked if he was happy to have a photo with us.

'Do I have to get up?' was his unenthusiastic response.

'Well, no, we'll get down with you,' I said as myself and Si clambered either side of him. I clumsily kicked sand over his towel and onto the open pages of his book.

'No, no, I'll get up!' he insisted whilst clearly trying to hide his frustration. Si cosied up close to him first for his souvenir picture whilst Jono was on photography duty. Afterwards, I went in, and threw an arm around Lineker.

Si then took the camera from Jono and insisted his less than enthusiastic brother take his turn.

Jono stood awkwardly next to Lineker, who was clearly wanting the event over as soon as possible to get back to his leisure time. Si, blissfully unaware of any urgency, shifted the camera left and right, changed from landscape to portrait and back again. When he finally had the shot he desired in his lens, he pressed what he assumed was the trigger button. At that point, the camera lens pulled in and the lens shutter slammed closed. He'd inadvertently turned the camera off. I didn't know whether to laugh or cry as he panicked to retrieve the situation and the two unwilling objects of the elusive photo shuffled further apart, both stood awkwardly still and visibly annoyed.

When the picture was finally taken, we wished Mr Lineker a good day. He afforded us a wry smile and wished us luck as we turned west, myself sniggering, Jono angrily embarrassed and Si trying to explain why he didn't know how to use his own camera.

When we arrived at the busiest section of the beach, it didn't disappoint: football, volleyball music, and vendors selling all manner of food, drink and local delicacies. The area is also famous for its surf as a constant, continuous series of ferocious waves crash onto the sand. It was great fun and replaced Copacabana as our regular daily venue of choice.

I had finally confirmed arrangements with Lorraine and successfully completed the purchase of the four tickets to the upcoming match at the Maracanã, which would now be a spicy all South American encounter between Uruguay and Colombia.

We were now so comfortable with our surroundings that we were casually walking the streets alone carrying cash and mobile phones. Lorraine, along with every other local resident we met, was lovely and the antithesis of the generalisations that had attempted to brainwash European travellers in the months leading up to the tournament. Lorraine immediately offered commiserations to me about the fact the game would not feature England and we shared a joke on the matter. In truth, the excitement to see a World Cup knockout match at the Maracanã had now dwarfed the disappointment over England's shortcomings.

There was, of course, only one choice for who would be offered the fourth and spare ticket. Sergio gleefully accepted and excitedly began planning the logistics for the day. His beloved Brazil were playing in the afternoon game and our match was in the evening. Sergio strategically planned us a route to take in one of his favourite bars for food, drinks and the early game before heading to the legendary stadium. We all decided to wear yellow in support of the host nation and also for Colombia, as both games would feature a fierce rivalry, against fellow South Americans in Chile and Uruguay respectively.

We arrived early and got seated in the porch area of the bar, directly in front of the big screen TV. We worked our way through the *cerveja* and a platter of Mexican food as hordes of locals gathered behind us. This, again, was not a tourist spot and some of the natives were clearly unimpressed that *gringos* (foreigners) had the best seats in the house whilst they jostled for viewing space. There were moments of unrest as the same guys, clearly unnerved by any confrontation, snarled and hissed at any Chile or Uruguay supporters that happened to pass.

The legion of yellow-shirted fanatics again went red-faced and wide-eyed as they shouted every word of their national anthem along with their heroes. The emotion was something to behold and I now hoped for a Brazil victory almost as much as I had dreamed of English glory.

As the superior team and host nation, Brazil were expected to beat Chile with a degree of comfort. Chile, however, were performing in the exact manner *técnico* Jorge Sampaoli instilled not only in his team but in himself: aggressive and energetic.

The teams were locked at one goal each as English referee Howard Webb blew his full-time whistle, signalling 30 minutes of extra time.

As the game had progressed, the crazed local supporters had realised we too were English and with every blow Howard Webb made of his whistle, they would either boo or cheer in our direction dependent on whether the decision was against or for their beloved nation. Any anxieties over their attitude towards us had lifted; they, like all their compatriots, were merely fun-loving if slightly over-passionate gentlemen.

The country had come to a standstill for this tournament and glory was not hoped for but expected. The nerves were palpable amongst the crowd around us, which mirrored the team on the pitch, who were playing as if they had the weight of not only the country on their shoulders but the whole world.

With seconds to go until the whistle sounded again, this time signalling the dreaded penalty shoot-out, Chile attacker Panilla latched onto the ball and thrashed it goalwards. It rocketed past veteran Brazilian *goleiro* Julio César and a gasp came from the anxious crowd before the ball rebounded back from the crossbar. I peered over my shoulder to witness a sea of faces, each with eyes and mouths open as wide as possible at the realisation that they had escaped what, at the time, to them was a fate worse than death.

The drama continued on the pitch and the tension intensified as the shoot-out went to sudden death, where each kick could mean disaster. Neymar calmly rolled the ball into the bottom corner. In contrast, experienced journeyman defender Jara Reyes was to take the decisive kick for Chile. It looked a perfect penalty as it arrowed towards the top corner of the net but cannoned across the face of the goal from the inside of the post.

It was relief on an unprecedented scale for the crowd surrounding us as they cried in one another's arms. The seemingly maniacal supporters of two hours ago now hugged and high-fived us as we bustled our way through them to continue our journey to the Maracanã.

As we approached the stadium the sun was disappearing behind the magnificent structure. Dozens of heavily armed guards were holding back hundreds of protesters; Sergio informed us this was due to the lavish spending of tax-payers' money for the tournament and corruption allegations which surrounded it.

The walkway spirals upwards around the circumference of the ground, calling in at a platform for entry to each seating level. It was a spine-tingling feeling as the pitch and surrounding stands came into view, and simultaneously a wall of noise and intensity hit us.

The yellow shirts vastly outnumbered the blue ones, largely due to the locals and neutrals, such as us, supporting the more popular Colombia team, who were now expected to beat the historically stronger Uruguay. This was principally down to the fact that Suarez, whilst living up to his reputation as a world-class footballer against England, had lived up to his reputation as a violent thug in the following match against Italy. For the third time in his career, Suarez had bitten an opponent during open play. Despite his denial and farcical yarn that he had tripped and merely fallen with his ample front teeth protruding from his face, directly into the shoulder of Italian defender Giorgio Chiellini, FIFA banned him for the remainder of the tournament and beyond.

In contrast, Colombian star James Rodríguez was not only available to play, but had been one of the stand-out performers of the entire *fase de grupos*.

We arrived at our seats and were surrounded by Colombia supporters; whether they were natives of the country or not was immaterial for the next two or three hours of sporting drama in this legendary amphitheatre. The general atmosphere in the majority of the stadium was jovial, whilst maintaining a raucous buzz of excitement. We had our England flag to show our allegiance and for a memorable photo opportunity (I had emblazoned it with our hometown team name 'Featherstone Colliery'). The Uruguay fans were in smaller, sporadic sections of the near 80,000 crowd.

Whilst the ticketing policy was fair and ensured packed-out stadia and tremendous atmospheres, the negative element was that opposition supporters would finish up shoulder to shoulder inside the stadia, due to the availability of 'neutral' area tickets sold on from the local residents who had been issued them in the ballot.

Even before the game started, the outnumbered blue-shirted fans were in a sinister mood. Objects were being thrown and they were aggressively taunting the Colombians.

The game got underway but I was more interested in the sights and sounds around me; as the sunlight disappeared and the bright lights of the Maracanã came into focus, the atmosphere was becoming tenser by the minute.

We were sat directly behind the goal that Colombia were attacking as they came forward with 28 minutes on the clock. The ball was looped towards star player Rodríguez 25 yards out with his back to goal. He took a minuscule glance over his shoulder to confirm where the target was, before guiding the ball to his right using his chest and then volleying it towards goal with as much power as he could muster. From my perspective, the ball was barely deviating, just getting larger as it arrowed towards us, and if it wasn't for the intervention of the underside of the crossbar as the ball crashed against it and downwards into the goal, it may well have sent our *cervejas* flying!

There was a momentary silence whilst the crowd gasped in amazement and processed what they had witnessed, before an eruption of sound that made the age-old foundations of the stadium vibrate. The strike went on to win the acclaimed Goal of the Tournament award.

Once the celebrations calmed, it quickly became apparent that there were scuffles and fights breaking out all around the stadium as the Uruguay supporters continued to throw missiles and even charge at any Colombia supporters in their reach. This continued through half-time and into the second half, five minutes into which Rodríguez claimed a second goal to almost confirm the first ever World Cup quarter-final for his country. The more jubilant the Colombia supporters got, the more repugnant the Uruguayan fans were in response. By now all the security guards were in the stands, making their best attempts to repel the waves of supporters launching themselves at each other with violent intent. The match all of a sudden became a side-show to the real event that was happening all around us.

Following the final whistle, it was a stampede to the exits and down the spiralling walkway. Brawls could be heard breaking out on the floors above and below us, but we strolled serenely out of the ground, luckily in amongst mostly fellow neutral supporters.

We had to get the subway back to Ipanema and Sergio needed to head in the opposite direction, so we said our goodbyes. That was the final time I saw Sergio, but we have become close friends from afar since then and converse very regularly.

So, it would be the impressive Colombia next up for the stumbling Brazil in the quarter-final encounter. We again attended The Jockey Club and, following their team's uninspiring performances, the anxiety of the masses had risen even further. But so had the enthusiasm; this was the *Copa do Mundo* quarter-final and *Hexacampeonato* was now in sight.

Another energetic and passionate rendition of the national anthem once again raised the nervous excitement. There was a release in the tension early though as *capitão* Thiago Silva scrambled the ball into the goal from a Neymar corner to give the *Canarinhos* the lead.

Popular frizzy-haired defender David Luiz doubled the advantage with a spectacular free kick in the second half.

Just after the hour mark, skipper Silva challenged Colombian *goleiro* David Ospina. The referee judged it a foul worthy of a yellow card, the second of the tournament for Silva, meaning he would serve a one-match suspension in the semi-final stage.

A Colombia penalty converted by their star player Rodríguez made for a nervous last ten minutes, but Brazil saw the victory out and had successfully navigated their way into the semi-final.

In the final moments however, as the ball bounced into the midriff of Neymar, Colombian defender Juan Zúñiga frustratedly launched himself with a raised knee into the lower back of the superstar. Neymar had to be stretchered off and taken to hospital, where scans showed he had cracked vertebrae. He would play no further part in the *Copa do Mundo*.

But that was a worry for tomorrow, as no group of people alive can party like those of Brazil following a World Cup knockout victory, and temporarily at least, we three were Brazilian.

The following morning we began our journey to Brasilia for the quarter-final match between Argentina and Belgium at the Mané Garrincha stadium. Named after the legendary player from the sixties, the previously dilapidated structure had been given a $900 million renovation; making it the second most expensive football stadium in the world behind Wembley.

We walked past newsagents and all the front pages of the newspapers were awash with the image of Neymar writhing in agony.

Aesthetically, the Mané Garrincha stadium was the finest I have ever seen or visited. Coliseum-like in its structure, it had a gladiatorial feel about it and the high, steep stands were vertigo-inducing.

The massive investment in the stadium had come ahead of not only the World Cup, but also the 2013 FIFA Confederations Cup and the 2016 Rio Olympic Games. Unfortunately, due to there being no local major *Brasileiro* club, it has been tragically underused and is now seen as a giant example of how the government mismanages the economy whilst so many of their citizens live in abject poverty. The total investment in stadia and infrastructure associated with the World Cup was estimated at a staggering $6 billion. As these figures appeared in the press in the months leading up to the tournament, social unrest grew.

Accusations of corruption were rife; where had all the money gone, whilst the majority of communities lived without hospitals and healthcare, without schools and education?

A campaign led by left-wing political activists gained momentum until protests and marches were almost constant. They grew violent and the protesters vowed to continue to wreak mayhem until the tournament was cancelled. Whilst they had been unsuccessful in that target, minor protests continued throughout the *Copa*, as we had witnessed approaching the Maracanã.

It turned into political and civil war. The government and tournament organisers told their people the *Copa* was for them. They promised that the *Canarinhos* would win the World Cup and avenge the 1950 final loss on home soil. They promised *Hexacampeonato*.

Brazil simply *must* win this tournament.

It was wonderful to see the precocious Lionel Messi in live action. To the irritation of the many natives in the stadium, their nemeses Argentina joined them in the final four, the match settled by an exquisite goal from Gonzalo Higuaín.

In an exciting semi-final stage; Brazil were to host three-time World Champions Germany in Belo Horizonte and Argentina would play Holland in São Paulo on 8 and 9 July respectively. Natives and neutrals alike began to dream of a Brazil versus Argentina final.

For this eagerly awaited *Canarinhos* match, we were going to an event being hosted at the Lagoa Stadium: a lavish structure that generally played host to water sports enthusiasts whilst events were taking place on the famous and picturesque lagoon.

A smaller venue meant far less people and we were lucky this was the first venue we had chosen that was indoor viewing. Lucky, because we were re-introduced to the Brazilian rain that had proved a terrible omen the day England were eliminated. It crashed down on the terracing roof and the hosts were soon giving out the clear plastic coats that Chapecó residents are so accustomed to.

The dark clouds were so thick that daylight had almost disappeared completely as the 5pm kick-off arrived. Wet clothes grew cold on the skin and the darkness felt eery; there were thoughts this was an omen yet again.

David Luiz led out the team as stand-in captain for the suspended Thiago Silva. The national anthem was slightly more muted than at previous matches as Luiz and *goleiro* Julio César held up the yellow jersey of Neymar throughout the song in honour of their fallen team-mate and hero.

118

Just ten minutes into the match, the mood worsened further as Germany took the lead. A few minutes later, sensing we were running low on *cerveja*, I told Si and Jono I would call to use the *banheiro*, then replenish the beer at the bar.

Stood in the small queue for the toilet, some young men were chatting away in Portuguese whilst keeping track of the score on their smart phones. Suddenly, they all looked to the heavens or put their hands to their faces in anguish. It was two to Germany.

Whilst using the toilet, I heard anguished, raised voices from behind me. I recognised one word well (as I had been asking for that number of beers so often for the previous four weeks) that kept being repeated: '*três*'. It was three.

I left the *banheiro* to join another small queue, this time at the bar. More anguish; this time it was more animated as those around me dropped to their knees into the pools of rainwater. Four. The atmosphere was turning surreal.

'*Três cerveja por favor*,' I said to the young chap behind the bar, who was trying to remain professional and courteous despite clearly feeling the same horror as his comrades. A smaller man with short dark hair was stood to my left, silently looking down at his mobile phone whilst waiting for some alcohol to quell his torment.

I then heard him quietly murmur, '*Cinco*.' Five. Then a little louder, '*Cinco!*' He then turned to face me, assuming I too was Brazilian due to my sopping *Canarinhos* jersey. He grabbed my shoulders and leaned in towards me, his face reddened and shaking, '*CINCO!*'

Less than 30 minutes of the game had passed and it was over. The dream was gone. *Hexacampeonato* would be a minimum of four years away. The 40-year unbeaten home record was obsolete. They would have to watch another nation lift the golden trophy they loved so much, and on their own shores, in their beloved Maracanã stadium. God forbid it be Argentina.

Sitting through the second half was a strange experience. Similar to being in a pub following a funeral. Very surreal.

Germany scored again. And again. Oscar managed a goal of tiny consolation to give a phenomenal final scoreline of one to the home side; seven to the visitors.

Uruguay 1950 had been the first of these national-depression-inducing catastrophic results: 32 years later, it was Italy 1982 which inspired Carlos Drummond de Andrade to write *Perder, Ganhar, Viver*. Now, 32 years on again, it was Germany 2014: the three footballing tragedies of Brazil.

Argentina beat Holland on a penalty shoot-out to enhance the tortured souls of Brazil and advance to the final.

The two losing semi-finalists always play off for the third-place medal. Neither team nor their supporters want to take part in this charade, but that has never been truer than for this Brazilian team. Their national humiliation meant they individually and collectively wanted to hide away and fly back to their distant European homes.

They were humiliated once more as the Dutch beat them 3–0.

'DEPRESSING' was the simple headline of *O Globo* the following morning; which was the day of the final they had hoped would be full of joy.

Brazilian football was broken; Brazil as a nation was broken too.

They were saved from the ultimate humiliation as Germany beat Argentina by the narrowest of margins to lift their fourth *Copa do Mundo*.

The day after the final, Luiz Felipe Scolari left his post. He was the seventh successive Brazil *técnico* to leave the role immediately after failing to bring home the coveted title of World Champions.

I left the country smitten with the happy and smiling people that live there, but with a heavy heart for the lives many are forced to live. I was particularly enamoured with their passionate relationship with *futebol* and the *Canarinhos* were now my undoubted second team in international football.

On my return home, I began to follow the results of the *Brasileiro*.

12

O Retorno

The return of the *Brasileiro* finally brought some *futebol* pain relief from the horror of the *Copa do Mundo*.

On 19 August, 43,000 fans were in attendance at the Estádio do Morumbi; home of *Série A* heavyweights São Paulo. They were all hoping to catch a glimpse of a returning hero.

For the home supporters, it was the legendary Kaká, who had returned to the club where he started his career before going on to conquer European football. In his outstanding career, he had won the World Cup in 2002 with the *Canarinhos* and multiple league titles in various countries. In 2007, whilst playing for AC Milan, Kaká won the European Champions League and the individual honours of FIFA World Player of the Year and the illustrious *Ballon d'Or*. He was going to spend his twilight years playing in American Major League Soccer for Orlando City, a franchise club yet to make their debut. Whilst awaiting the start of the next campaign in the USA, Kaká had romantically signed a contract to play the remainder of the *Brasileiro* season with his beloved São Paulo.

For the away supporters, it was the one and only Bruno Rangel, who would make his first appearance in *Série A* at the age of 32 and pull on the green shirt of Chape for the first time in eight months.

Celso Rodrígues again deployed them in the typical defensive way, knowing they were against technically superior individuals and a team near the top of the standings. But the team contained the likes of Danilo in goal as well as Neném and Rangel in a line-up that felt much more akin with the Big Green the fans knew and loved.

São Paulo had ten attempts at goal to the three of Chape, ten corner kicks to the five of the away team and 63 per cent possession of the ball. But in true mastery of the *Era Parreira* tactics and inspired by their own returning hero, the Big Green won 1–0: their first away win in *Série A*.

Chape continued their tour of the giants of the state of São Paulo seven days later when they visited sixth-placed Santos at the Estádio Vila Belmiro.

During the 1960s, Santos were regarded as the Harlem Globetrotters of football. They had a host of the legendary skilful players who were representing Brazil during their golden era, including the greatest player of all time: Pelé. They dominated Brazilian, South American and world club football. Known as the *Santásticos,* they were in demand worldwide and became globetrotters in their own right, travelling far and wide to perform in exhibition matches. On one occasion, a war in Africa was stopped so that the two sides could watch Pelé and his team-mates perform *O Jogo Bonito.*

In the decades since, with a much smaller stadium and budget, Santos had been overtaken by many of the other major *Série A* clubs. But they had brought through Neymar Jr. and the riches created from his sale to Barcelona just one year earlier in the summer of 2013 had rejuvenated the club and strengthened the squad.

They beat Chape 3–0.

Of the population of approximately 200 million, over 30 million people in Brazil are supporters of Flamengo – considerably the largest fan base in the country. Their original home, the Estádio da Gávea, was just one mile away from the apartment I lived in for five weeks during the *Copa do Mundo.* We walked past it on a regular basis. It is emblazoned with the club crest and the famous red and black colours. It looks sentimentally historic and ancient. The decorative exterior features old-fashioned painted artwork rather than the modern computer-produced, electronically lit signage. With just one main stand, it has a capacity of only

4,000. Therefore, as their popularity grew and grew through the decades, they began using the Maracanã for their biggest home games until 1997, when it became their official home ground for all matches and the Estádio da Gávea became a relic, used for lower key matches such as those of the ladies and youth teams.

I was unaware of this and assumed the small, antiquated stadium I was seeing up close so regularly was in fact the home ground of the famous Flamengo. I bought myself the club jersey and other merchandise and designated them my *Brasileiro* team, and the club whose results I would follow from afar on my *retorno* home.

Less than three weeks after landing back in England, in early August, I did indeed check the latest result of my new team. I knew they were struggling near the bottom of the standings, but to my shock, they had lost 1–0 to a team I had never even heard of; that team was Associação Chapecoense de Futebol.

Defender Rafael Lima had scored an extremely rare goal early in the match to the delight of the majority of the 13,000 supporters at the Arena Condá. It proved enough for a Chape victory and for them to move up to 12th place in *Série A*. He celebrated wildly with the adoring fans, grabbing the club crest on his jersey and pounding it into his heart.

The defensive, hard-working style of play was working and the Big Green were gaining a reputation for being an uncomfortable team to play against and a tough team to break down. And so, the low-scoring, close encounters continued:

Chapecoense	1 – 1	Atlético Mineiro
Chapecoense	0 – 1	Figueirense
Vitória	0 – 0	Chapecoense
Chapecoense	1 – 0	Fluminense
Botafogo	1 – 0	Chapecoense

Since the return of the *Brasileiro* and that of Bruno Rangel, Chape had scored only four goals in the eight matches and Bruno had failed to strike once. Chances at goal for the team were so few, confidence was spiralling downwards. Results were beginning to suffer.

Next up was a visit to the league leaders, defending champions and the undisputed current top team: Cruzeiro, of Belo Horizonte.

Just ten minutes into the match, knowing chances would be scarce, Chape midfielder Dedé took a speculative shot from over 30 yards. It struck his team-mate Zezinho on the ankle and deflected into the goal. To the shock of the 27,000-strong crowd, Chape had taken an early lead, one that they would hold on to and take into the half-time interval.

Early in the second half though, Cruzeiro showed they were indeed a class apart from little Chapecoense: Danilo had to collect the ball out of his goal three times in an eight-minute onslaught by the champions. He had only conceded that same number of goals in the previous five matches combined.

Forced into a more attacking style, with 20 minutes to go, a good opportunity finally fell for Bruno Rangel, who clinically dispatched the ball into the goal to end his drought. Approaching his 33rd birthday, he was finally a goalscorer in the top flight of Brazilian football. He followed the ball into the back of the goal to collect it in a bid to get the game restarted as soon as possible, in the hope of completing the sensational comeback; therefore his adoring supporters had still not seen his trademark goal celebration.

The match ended in a defeat by four goals to two.

A week later it was back to the attritional campaign in another goalless draw at the Arena Condá, this time against Goiás.

This marked the halfway stage of the season; Chape had played each *Série A* team once and were in an unlikely position of survival, but would have to negotiate the second part of the season in a similar manner.

Brasileiro Série A standings; September 2014 (bottom six)

#	Team	GP	P
15	Chapecoense	19	20
16	Palmeiras	19	18
17	Criciúma	19	18
18	Coritiba	19	17
19	Bahia	19	17
20	Vitória	19	15

GP = Games Played
P = Points

Just five of the 20 points accumulated by Chape had been achieved away from the Arena Condá. Chapecó had gained the respect of *Série A* with the battling and defensive style of Chape coupled with the incessant rain that seemed to await the next visitors. It had quickly gotten a reputation as an extremely uncomfortable 90 minutes for even the most gifted of players and teams.

The terrible form on the road continued in game 20 as the Big Green were beaten comprehensively by relegation rivals Coritiba, and the two teams were suddenly on identical points. A simultaneous Palmeiras victory sank Chape to just one place above the trapdoor.

Bottom club Vitória had fired their experienced *técnico* Jorginho a few weeks earlier and so the Chapecoense board of directors took the opportunity to hire him as the new head coach; Celso Rodrígues and Anderson Paixão would return to their roles as assistant coach and fitness trainer respectively.

The pressure was on continuing to get good home results to rescue Chape as they welcomed seventh-placed Sport Recife to the Arena Condá.

As is always the prerogative of a new coach, Jorginho made a host of changes to the team. Five players lost their places; among them was Bruno Rangel, who had scored just one goal in 11 appearances since his return.

Rangel was replaced by 23-year-old new recruit Leandro Pereira, who had impressed in his cameo displays from the substitutes' bench. Yet another player plucked from the wastelands of the lower echelons of the system.

Without the yet again injured Neném and with Nivaldo and Rangel seemingly past their best and replaced in the starting team by younger athletes, once again the Chape team had an unfamiliar feel to it.

But the young stars rose to the occasion and rallied to a spectacular performance and a victory by three goals to one. The young *atacante* Pereira assisted two of the goals and was named Man of the Match.

Bruno Rangel didn't even make it off the substitutes' bench, and there was a feeling that his *retorno* was not going to be anywhere near as magical as his first term. Maybe his ageing body was just too old to be stepping up to *Série A* for the first time.

New *técnico* Jorginho had been so impressed with the performance he kept almost the same starting line-up for the upcoming matches:

Corinthians	1 – 1	Chapecoense
Grémio	1 – 0	Chapecoense
Chapecoense	3 – 0	Atlético Paranaense
Chapecoense	1 – 1	Criciúma
Palmeiras	4 – 2	Chapecoense

Despite the continued sense of overachievement that had now been ongoing for several years, Chape were still only one position outside the bottom four relegation places of *Série A*.

Week 27 brought Internacional back to the Arena Condá for the first time since the 2008 *Copa do Brasil* encounter which had been one of the key events to spark the financial and sporting reversal in the fortunes of Associação Chapecoense de Futebol. Again, there was a friendly face in the red jersey of their opponents for many of the players and staff as popular full-back Alan Ruschel returned to Chapecó.

The Big Green went into the match having lost just one of their previous ten home matches and having won six in that period. But Internacional arrived as the second-best team in Brazil: only the all-conquering Cruzeiro ahead of them in the standings.

Stood inside the opposite goal of Danilo was the legendary Dida, a man with 91 appearances for the *Canarinhos* and a winners' medal from the 2002 World Cup. During his 23-year career, split equally between the *Brasileiro* and Italian giants AC Milan, Dida had won almost everything the sport had to offer.

With over 17,000 supporters inside the stadium cheering on their heroes, with a confidence in their home form, with the players' and staff members' families together inside the ground, with faith in their defenders, with Danilo in goal, Chape allowed Internacional to have most of the possession and with the young, quick attacking players, they struck quickly on the counter-attack. To the shock and delight of everyone associated with the club, they struck time after time and in a match that will live forever in the minds of the Chapecoense supporters, they beat the mighty Internacional 5–0. In the final few minutes, the embarrassed and frustrated Dida had been sent off, forcing an outfield team-mate to put on his goalkeeping jersey to finish the match.

It was a result that completed the amazing rise of Chape from the encounter only six years earlier on the same pitch, when it had seemed inconceivable that they could compete with a club the size of Internacional. Now they had humiliated them.

The confidence from this game continued and manifested into a rare away victory, 1–0 over relegation rivals Bahia. Once again Chape had absorbed pressure from the opposition, Danilo repelling seven strikes on his goal to secure the victory which lifted his team to 13th in the league table: four places and four points ahead of the relegation zone with ten games remaining.

Chape weren't scoring many goals, but almost all the ones they were managing were coming from Leandro Pereira, as the young replacement for Bruno Rangel continued to excel. It was looking more and more as though Bruno should have stayed in Qatar and earned some life-changing money, rather than making the emotional and heartfelt return.

Despite the lofty position, no one associated with the club was feeling calm with regards to the dream of *Série A* survival, as each of the next five fixtures were against teams above them in the standings:

Atlético Mineiro	1 – 0	Chapecoense
Chapecoense	0 – 0	São Paulo
Chapecoense	1 – 1	Santos
Flamengo	3 – 0	Chapecoense
Figueirense	1 – 0	Chapecoense

Brasileiro Série A standings; 9 November 2014 (bottom six)

#	Team	GP	P
15	Coritiba	33	37
16	Chapecoense	33	36
17	Vitória	33	34
18	Botafogo	33	33
19	Bahia	33	31
20	Criciúma	33	30

Five matches without a victory had brought the club and *técnico* Jorginho under pressure once more. But the reprieve that had always been on the horizon had arrived in the form of a home match against Vitória.

Chape had not lost a match at the Arena Condá for three months; Vitória were a place below them in the league; Jorginho had been the opposition's coach for the first half of the campaign and so would surely know their strengths, weaknesses and tactics.

It was role reversal for the Chape players as they had most of the ball and more goal opportunities than their opponents, but could not make the breakthrough in a game that lacked any quality. With the match into the final ten minutes it appeared both teams had settled for a point each, which would leave them very much alive in the battle for survival, when a Vitória midfielder hopefully put the ball into the Chapecoense penalty area. It fell to striker Dinei, who creatively back-heeled it to his team-mate before peeling away from the Big Green defender. Simultaneously, the team-mate played the ball back into the stride of Dinei in a fantastic footballing manoeuvre to create a very rare opportunity in the match. Dinei clinically thrashed the ball beyond Danilo to complete a brilliant and unexpected goal. The match finished 1–0 to the away team and plunged Chape into the dreaded bottom four for the first time since before the break for the World Cup and with just four games remaining to save themselves.

Brasileiro Série A standings; 17 November 2014 (bottom six)

#	Team	GP	P
15	Vitória	34	37
16	Coritiba	34	37
17	Chapecoense	34	36
18	Botafogo	34	33
19	Bahia	34	31
20	Criciúma	34	30

The Chapecoense football bosses of Sandro Pallaoro, João Carlos Maringá, Cadu Gaúcho and Mauro Stumpf made the decision to terminate the contract of Jorginho despite him having had only 14 matches in the post, and reinstate the temporary coaching team of Celso Rodrígues and Anderson Paixão for the crucial final four games of the campaign.

The first of these vital matches was against Fluminense of Rio de Janeiro, who also play their home games at the iconic Maracanã stadium alongside their intensely hated rivals Flamengo.

Fluminense were in seventh position and expected a victory to keep alive their hopes of finishing in the lucrative top four positions that would give them access to the 2015 *Copa Libertadores*: the South American equivalent of the European Champions League.

Neném was back from his injury but Celso Rodrígues kept him and Bruno Rangel on the substitutes' bench alongside Nivaldo as the three legendary veterans continued to make way for the younger athletes.

The most recent result had plunged Chape to the cusp of relegation and the media had once again depicted them as beyond hope of survival. With the team yet again without a permanent *técnico*, highly respected football director Maringá gave a pre-match speech to the team in which he implored them to ignore outside voices predicting the result. He told them he believed in them, and that the opposition were just 11 men with two feet each, just the same as them. Finally, he told them that he didn't just believe they would beat Fluminense inside the Maracanã, but he knew they would beat them well, by a big scoreline.

For the second time in just a few short weeks, the Big Green stars walked out onto the hallowed turf of the Maracanã. A crowd of 30,000 was in attendance. Just one month earlier they had been comprehensively beaten by Flamengo inside the same stadium.

Chapecoense began the match as they always did when up against technically superior opposition. They allowed Fluminense to have the majority of possession. But once more, Marcos Danilo Padilha was purely inspired. He made multiple awe-inspiring saves to keep the scoreline goalless at half-time.

Just moments after the match restarted, the ball made a rare appearance in the Fluminense penalty area. Confusion between the previously inactive defensive players saw the ball break to Chape midfielder Camilo who drilled a shot towards goal through a sea of Fluminense defenders. No matter how many times you see the video, it is almost impossible to comprehend how the ball made it through the non-existent gap in the block of contorted torsos and limbs. But it did. And then it crashed into the goal, almost bursting a hole in the netting. The Chapecoense players sprinted to the team dugout to celebrate with the likes of Bruno Rangel, Nivaldo and Neném.

From that moment on, with the Fluminense players shell-shocked and unable to pick themselves up from the most surprising of deficits, their green-clad opposition became inspired like they had been against Internacional. They attacked swiftly, precisely, clinically. The hugely partisan Rio crowd were silenced as Chape ripped their team apart and scored time and again for another famous victory.

Just three days later Chape faced a seemingly simpler task when they welcomed a team for whom relegation was nearing certainty to the Arena Condá. Unfortunately for my friend Sergio, that team was his beloved Botafogo.

A victory by two goals to nil sent Chapecoense four points clear of the relegation zone with just two games remaining and six points to play for. The outstanding Leandro Pereira again scored both goals as he proved the salvation for the Big Green. But the performance came as the big *clubes* of *Série A* had already begun to circulate, and were now ready to pounce. Both Corinthians Paulista and Palmeiras made offers for his signature and Chapecoense would be powerless to prevent a move happening.

Another discovery from obscurity by Cadu Gaúcho had all but guaranteed the club's *Série A* survival, and was now about to be transferred to a major team, and in the process make ACF another healthy profit to be reinvested.

In the penultimate round of matches, Chape would play on the Sunday, with Vitória – their rivals for the final *rebaixamento* place – in action on the Saturday evening. Ironically, Vitória were now the ones going to the Maracanã in need of a victory as they faced an away match against in-form Flamengo. A defeat would mean their relegation to *Série B* and confirm an amazing survival for Chape.

The Chapecoense family, with eager anticipation of the result, gathered to watch the game together in the bar of the Hotel Bertaso, which had not only been the venue of the crisis meeting which had saved the club, but had also become a second home for

Chapecoense. They meet there, eat there, socialise there and stay overnight there to prepare for big games.

On this occasion the tension was lifted with less than 30 minutes on the clock as Flamengo took the lead, signalling the launch of wild celebrations in Chapecó, both inside and out of the Hotel Bertaso.

As the match progressed and Flamengo scored goal after goal against their beleaguered opposition, the realisation began that Chapecoense had achieved the impossible survival and had done so with two games to spare.

Fittingly, following the scenes of celebration, the Arena Condá hosted runaway champions Cruzeiro. Both teams had already accomplished their respective targets for the campaign, so the match was a purely joyous occasion for all the players, management and supporters alike.

Celso Rodrígues selected Bruno Rangel from the start, as Leandro Pereira had agreed a move to Palmeiras; he had played his final game for Chapecoense.

After the pouring rains that had helped Chape grind out the results in their home stadium for most of the season, now, with the result of less importance and the pure enjoyment of those in the stadium coming to the fore, it was a sunny day in Chapecó. The players were urged to go and express themselves and enjoy the occasion, with far less emphasis on the *Era Parreira* tactics.

Late in the first half, with the score still goalless, Chape stalwart Wanderson drove into the penalty area and managed to squeeze the ball across the face of the goal and into the path of his friend Bruno Rangel, who smashed it into the net to give his team a sensational lead over the champions elect. He peeled away and sprinted towards the overjoyed supporters, looking and pointing both index fingers skyward before dropping to his knees as his comrades swarmed around him in the familiar celebration the supporters had not seen for a year. It was his second *Série A* goal, and both had come against the mighty Cruzeiro.

Into the second half, the crowd waved flags, sang songs and performed Mexican waves. To their further delight, Celso Rodrígues made a rare substitution as he brought on the Eternal Nivaldo for his top-flight bow at 40 years of age, joining his friend

Neném as only the second player to appear at every level of the *Brasileiro*. Marcos Danilo Padilha made way and was given a standing ovation as he left the field of play.

The match ended in a draw. It was the final game of the season at the Arena Condá and the players were joined in celebration by their families as their young children came onto the pitch to wave in gratitude to the loyal supporters.

The final match of the long and arduous campaign saw Nivaldo, Neném and Bruno Rangel all once again deployed and the defensive handbrake continued to be lifted as Chape lost 4–2 against Goiás.

However, Bruno did complete his return to form with another goal; he had done enough to prove he still had what was required to compete at the high standard.

Brasileiro Série A 2014 final standings (bottom six)

#	Team	GP	P
15	Chapecoense	38	43
16	Palmeiras	38	40
17	Vitória	38	38
18	Bahia	38	37
19	Botafogo	38	34
20	Criciúma	38	32

Despite the many coaching changes, the team of football directors, João Carlos Maringá, Cadu Gaúcho and Mauro Stumpf, supported by President Sandro Pallaoro, had now guided the team from *Série D* to a second consecutive season in *Série A*.

Maringá had delivered an instrumental speech before the crucial match against Fluminense and did so, more than anyone wanting the team to survive, as he had decided to leave his role and desperately wanted to walk away from the club he loved with them still a member of the top flight. And he did.

Whilst holding onto *Série A* status was the one and only objective and that had been accomplished, the surprising success brought with it an additional bonus; qualification for the South American *Copa Sul Americana* 2015. Associação Chapecoense de Futebol would now be competing internationally against some of the major teams of the whole continent.

Individually and collectively, the players and the team were achieving more than they had imagined possible. As John F. Kennedy once said, 'A rising tide lifts all boats.'

13

Histórico

I reached out to many sources when researching this book. I made attempts through social media to speak to players and staff, past or present, to supporters and family members: anyone associated with Chape during the decade in question.

Many never saw my initial ice-breaking message, due to various privacy settings and such like. Some saw but probably assumed my claims to be an author couldn't be true given the fact I was writing to them in almost nonsensical Portuguese that I was getting from a translating application. Anyone still directly associated with the club seemed to scare off easily; I believe they feared a conflict of interest.

One particular gentleman responded and seemed enamoured with my project and, after some opening communications through my two-way translator, I saved his details for when I would require the information for his part of the story.

His name is Vinícius Eutropio, and he was hired as head coach of Associação Chapecoense de Futebol almost immediately after the miraculous survival of 2014. Now an established *Série A* club, Chape would not only compete in the state championship and the top league of Brazil, they would also play in the national knockout tournament, *Copa do Brasil*, and the South American international competition, *Copa Sul Americana*. To be able to fulfil this extra burden on the schedule, a much bigger squad of players would be required.

Vinicius informed me that Chapecoense had been a team that, historically, had always hired players from the second and third divisions of Brazil. So when, in 2014, they reached the first division of the *Brasileiro,* they encountered many difficulties. They were almost relegated to the second division of both the state championship and to *Série B,* so he was hired on 14 December 2014.

The following day he introduced himself in a meeting arranged to set up the 2015 squad. At the three-hour-long meeting he gave a presentation to President Pallaoro, Vice-President Mauro Stumpf and football director Cadu Gaúcho, insisting that he needed them to acquire the massive amount of 20 established *Série A* players, all between 25 and 30 years old, and they must be high-quality individuals both on and off the field.

'They got scared and called me crazy,' Vinícius told me.

They had just a few days to find and hire the players. All involved worked hard, and the heavy recruitment period was successful.

With the large squad put together and with so many new faces, Vinícius talked to all the players and explained that there could be problems early on, as the squad needed time to evolve. They all agreed they would not let their heads bow if there was a spell of bad results. They all also knew that with the much bigger squad, they would have to spend some matches sitting on the substitutes' bench. Vinícius told them they were the group that would be starting and finishing the long and arduous campaign ahead. Togetherness was his mantra.

Almost all of the players brought in were free transfers and loan deals for the rarely utilised squad members from the big clubs of *Série A.* Two examples of players who arrived on permanent contracts were Hélio Zampier Neto, an imposing 29-year-old, 6ft 5in defender with a piercing stare, and experienced, classy midfielder Cléber Santana, who earlier in his career had played in the European Champions League during a three-year spell at Atlético Madrid. Vinícius installed Santana as his *capitão.*

Following a disappointing third-place finish in the *Campeonato Catarinense,* President Pallaoro held his promise not to resort to yet another change of *técnico,* or to panic-buy yet more players to replace the individuals that had so far failed to deliver their finest form. Patience in the project worked and, sensationally, at the mid-point of the *Série A* season, Chapecoense were sat in ninth position.

'We were a family on the field and off the field, with many encounters with the children and the wives,' said Vinícius, whose team were making headlines in the national media.

The most amazing result came at the end of June, when Chape travelled to the two-time consecutive and defending champions Cruzeiro and came back to Chapecó triumphant.

Vinícius Eutropio had claimed victory over famous coach Vanderlei Luxemburgo, a former *técnico* of the Brazil national team and of the mighty Real Madrid.

But, if it is possible, the team were almost doing too well and, when Chape subsequently went six matches without victory, Vinícius became a victim of his own success.

'[In] the Brazilian championship, [there] are 38 games and Brazil is the size of all of Europe. This becomes almost impossible to keep on top all of the time, especially for a team that was set up in no time.

'Also we changed the way the team played, because [teams] in the south of the country and Chapecoense played with players stronger and with much marking. I play soccer lighter and more offensive.'

Vinícius began to tell me how and why his team started having problems, and how, after a home loss to Flamengo, he was asked to leave his role at the Arena Condá.

'This is football in Brazil.'

With some sadness, emotion and regret, Eutropio told me he had a great relationship with all of the players, but highlighted three members of his squad: Cléber Santana 'my *capitão*', Danilo and Bruno Rangel.

To highlight the warmth of the club, he told me how he substituted Nivaldo onto the field during a 3–0 win against Ponte Preta in the *Copa Sul Americana*, so that he became the only player ever to play in all four Brazilian divisions and a South American continental competition.

It was in the middle of September, following a defeat to Flamengo and after a run of six games without victory, that it was decided a change of coach was required once again. The Big Green were in 13th position in the league and had beaten Ponte Preta and advanced to the last 16 of the *Copa Sul Americana* under Vinícius Eutropio. They were scheduled to play in one of the biggest matches in their history just one week after his departure.

Bruno Rangel was still at the club. He was being used sparingly due to his advancing years, but was back in clinical goalscoring form; at this stage of the season, only four players in the whole of *Série A* had bettered his tally of eight, despite his limited time spent on the field of play.

An additional reason for showing the overachieving Vinícius Eutropio the exit door at the Arena Condá – apart from reinvigorating the squad that had looked lacklustre for a month – was that a highly sought-after *técnico* was readily available. That was Guto Ferreira, a 51-year-old coach who had enhanced his reputation by achieving promotion to *Série A* via a second-place finish in *Série B* with Ponte Preta and gaining qualification to the *Copa Sul Americana*.

Coincidentally, Chape had subsequently eliminated Preta from the *Copa Sul Americana* before hiring their former coach to replace Eutropio.

Fluminense wanted Ferreira and offered him a contract, only to find Chape had beaten them to his signature by a matter of hours. A perfectly timed Cadu Gaúcho telephone call to Ferreira, who he had known for many years, had secured his services.

The first game under the new *técnico* took Chape to play away against São Paulo. He predictably reverted to the *Era Parreira* tactics of old in hope of scraping a draw from the famous Morumbi stadium. This was achieved as the result was goalless.

However, a 2–0 home defeat to champions Cruzeiro meant it was now eight *Série A* games without victory.

The first leg of the eagerly awaited *Copa Sul Americana* last-16 tie arrived, as the Big Green embarked on an 800-mile bus journey to play Libertad, of Paraguay. Despite conceding an extremely late goal, Chape were happy to return with a 1–1 draw, including a crucial away goal.

Just three days later in the hectic schedule, was an away match against Sport Recife, which brought with it a 2,000-

mile flight. The terrible form of Chape continued as they were comprehensively beaten by three goals to nil. Despite their fantastic start to the season, Chapecoense had now fallen into the relegation positions.

Brasileiro Série A standings; 28 September 2015 (bottom six)

#	Team	GP	P
15	Avaí	28	32
16	Goiás	28	31
17	Chapecoense	28	31
18	Figueirense	28	28
19	Vasco	28	26
20	Joinville	28	24

GP = Games Played

P = Points

Rumours began that many supporters were planning to gather as a large group at the airport as the team returned to greet the misfiring stars with boos and jeers. New Vice-President Mauro Stumpf, who had taken promotion to the role following the departure of Maringá, heard about this and was worried it could wipe out any remaining confidence the squad had, and effectively confirm there would not be a second successive survival in the top division.

Stumpf managed to make contact with some of the key organisers of the fan protest and pleaded with them to change their agenda by telling them, 'When you have someone sick in the family, do you criticise or give them support to get them back on their feet? I need you there at the airport supporting and taking care of the players, who are also very upset by this defeat.'

As the players, coaches and staff prepared to leave the airport terminal, they could see that a crowd had formed and began to fear a barrage of abuse. But instead they were welcomed with cheers, chants and songs of support.

Four days later, Libertad were welcomed to the Arena Condá for the extremely tense second leg in the *Copa Sul Americana*, with a quarter-final place on the line.

The stadium was full on a dark Friday evening. The advantage gained from the scoring of an away goal one week earlier was lost after just four minutes when Libertad headed past the despairing Danilo.

Another four minutes past until the match was once again deadlocked: Cléber Santana cleverly chipped a free kick to the edge of the penalty area where Melo brilliantly thrashed a low volley into the goal.

A two-legged tie such as this can only go to the dreaded penalty shoot-out if both games have the same result, due to the away goals rule. And so it proved, as after a nervy period when both teams knew a goal concession would surely see their elimination, the referee finally blew the whistle to signify a shoot-out would be required.

First up for Chape, their penalty-taker extraordinaire, Bruno Rangel, who confidently brushed the ball into the bottom corner of the goal to give his team the first advantage. He jogged to the side of the goal where he and Danilo shared a celebratory embrace as the *goleiro* made his way to guard the net for his team-mates.

As the Libertad striker López prepared to take his kick, the confident and charismatic Danilo was pointing to the top corner of the goal whilst jumping from side to side on the goal line. He was goading the kicker into taking on an overly ambitious attempt, making him believe he already knew where he was aiming.

Mind games.

López did indeed strike the ball high towards the corner which Danilo had indicated. But he struck it too high and the ball sailed over the crossbar and into the raucous and delighted Chapecoense supporters. Danilo spun around and screamed with delight in their direction, his clenched fists punching the air.

With Danilo knelt at the goal side, eyes closed and pointing skywards in prayer, one by one his Big Green team-mates including Neto and *capitão* Santana, confidently made the net bulge. All five Chape marksmen converted to send the whole stadium into jubilant celebration.

Associação Chapecoense de Futebol were amongst the final eight teams of the coveted international tournament where they would play the famous, rich and glamorous River Plate of Buenos Aires, Argentina; defending champions of the *Copa Sul Americana*.

The long wait without a victory had technically continued, as they had drawn both home and away matches against Libertad. But the confidence was reinvigorated into the team. The support of their fans whilst they had been at their lowest had been repaid by taking the proud citizens of Chapecó on a South American adventure they never thought possible.

Just two days later the Arena Condá once again hosted Palmeiras. The São Paulo giants were placed fourth in the standings and in fine form. Chapecoense, on the other hand, had fallen freely down the league and were now inside the dreaded bottom four positions.

After just five minutes, giant defender Hélio Neto rose to power a headed goal and give the Big Green a shock lead.

Another of the bewilderingly brilliant performances that Chape were beginning to become synonymous with was about to happen. Yet again they gave the loyal supporters an evening to remember forever. They ended a nine-game winless streak by destroying their superstar opponents by an amazing five goals to one.

Week 30 of the 2015 *Série A* took Chape on the road to Rio once again, this time for a relegation scrap against the penultimately positioned team in the division: Vasco de Gama.

A draw would be a positive result for Chape, who had regained their status outside the bottom four clubs with the sensational performance over Palmeiras. Vasco needed a victory to gain ground on their rivals.

Predictably, it was a tight, low-quality match and Chape found themselves a goal down with only seven minutes remaining. This was when Guto Ferreira decided to put Bruno Rangel onto the pitch. The timing was perfect, as just three minutes later the referee saw an infringement inside the Vasco goalmouth and instantly pointed for a penalty kick: the speciality of Rangel.

With the pressure immeasurably high, once again Bruno appeared as calm and carefree as ever. He placed the ball on the spot, walked back and casually awaited the whistle of the referee. Once that arrived, he jogged up to the stationary ball before inevitably and clinically dispatching it into the bottom corner of the goal.

Once again Bruno Rangel had salvaged a crucial result for his team and the supporters that worshipped him.

The relentless schedule would continue and just three days later Chape made the short visit to the neighbouring state of Rio Grande do Sol to play the giants of Grêmio, who were in third place in *Série A*.

In the final seconds of the previous match Danilo had picked up a yellow card which, added to the ones he had already been shown through the season, meant he would serve a one-match suspension and miss the game against Grêmio.

Not wanting to be reliant on 41-year-old *goleiro* Nivaldo, Guto Ferreira opted to give young reserve goalkeeper Silvio his first start for the club and his debut in *Série A*.

After just five minutes, Silvio was called into action to deal with a long-range, powerful strike. Whilst it was travelling at speed and heading high into the net, it was straight down the middle of the goal and should've been dealt with quite comfortably. But, clearly feeling the pressure of the occasion in front of 20,000 spectators, Silvio misjudged the flight of the ball and allowed it to go through his arms and already Chape found themselves behind. Already they missed Danilo.

The Big Green were playing well in search of an equalising goal but ten minutes before half-time Grêmio attacked once more, which led to another misjudgment by the young *goleiro*. This time he palmed a low cross into an onrushing attacker, who scored having barely known how it had happened. The goalscorer had collided with young Silvio, who stayed down in some discomfort and needed treatment from the Chape physiotherapist.

Whether the injury or his mistakes were the reason, we cannot be sure, but Guto Ferreira substituted the stricken youngster for a man at the opposite end of his career: the Eternal Nivaldo.

In the second half, with nothing to lose, Chape attacked with lawless abandon and subsequently left gaping holes in their usually sound defence. There was chance after chance at both ends, but Nivaldo was rolling back the years, repelling attacks on his goal with relative ease. His opposite number, however, was not having such a strong game and with ten minutes of the match remaining, Chape had sensationally levelled the scoreline at two goals each. Captain Cléber Santana was dominating the midfield and controlling the play.

Due to many stoppages in the game, the officials had indicated a minimum of five minutes would be added on at the end. All Chapecoense wanted to do was hold on for the most unlikely of points. As the clock struck 94 minutes Chape had just soaked up another attack and Grêmio had thrown almost all their players forward in search of the victory they needed to keep themselves in the hunt for the *Série A* title. The ball arrived at the feet of Cléber Santana, who with typical calm allowed one of the few remaining defensive Grêmio players to rush towards him in the hope of dispossessing the Big Green *capitão*. Santana feigned to pass short to his right before skilfully dragging the ball left and past the defender. The whole pitch opened up ahead of him as he carried the ball over the halfway line. Finding energy where no one else could after almost 100 minutes of play was Chape defender Apodi, who sprinted with all his might to give his captain support. Santana played the ball with optimum timing into the stride of the surprising *atacante*, who was now bearing down on goal. Like an expert striker he confidently dispatched the ball past the despairing *goleiro* and into the bottom corner of the goal to initiate yet more scenes of unbridled joy and celebration for the Chape players, coaches, management and the travelling supporters that made up the minority in attendance; the majority were silent and dumbfounded.

Since reaching their lowest point following the terrible defeat at Recife, when their supporters gave them a standing ovation at the airport on their return, Chape had gained seven points from three extremely tough games to make a second successive survival in the top league of Brazil look extremely likely once again. They had also advanced to the quarter-finals of the *Copa Sul Americana*, and would be heading to Buenos Aires for the first duel with the mighty River Plate next.

It was a cold night in the Estadio Monumental. But a packed 65,000-capacity stadium, full with the violently passionate Argentina supporters, made the blood flow warm through the bodies of the Chapecoense stars.

It was Argentina versus Brazil. There was a semi-final place at stake over the two legs. The atmosphere was ferocious. For the players of River Plate, this was nothing new, they were the defending champions of this very competition. For the likes of Marcos Danilo Padilha, who little over two years ago was effectively out of work and wondering where his next pay cheque was coming from, this was very new indeed.

Despite performing well, Chape lost by three goals to one, but had scored a memorable and potentially vital away goal.

Seven days later the Arena Condá would host the reverse fixture. The streets of Chapecó were awash with frenzied supporters hoping for a glimpse of their heroes as the team bus made its way to the stadium. The dark sky was alight as an array of green flares were lit; flags were waved; songs and chants were sung. Chapecoense were now amongst the big time. The people of the city were proud and thankful for the journey they had been on and were out in force to show the team their feelings.

When the bus finally arrived after the extremely slow journey from the Hotel Bertaso, the squad disembarked and had to battle through the adoring public. The stars waved and smiled and posed. Mobbed most of all, were their *dueses*: Danilo and Bruno Rangel.

Knowing the vociferous support of the crowd would be crucial if they were to overturn the deficit, Guto Ferreira picked the team he knew the supporters would want to see. This meant rare starting berths for popular veterans Neném and Rangel. Neném now joined his friend Nivaldo as the only men to have played in every level of the *Brasileiro* and in a continental competition.

The whole country were behind Chape; any victory over an Argentinian team was sought after, nationwide. Before the match kicked off, as the players emerged from the tunnel and out onto grass, the atmosphere reached fever pitch.

Astonishingly, Bruno Rangel rolled back the years as he scored two goals to send the supporters into delirium. The score was 2–1 to Chape on the night and 4–3 to River Plate on aggregate and the tension was almost unbearable as Chape swept forward in search of the goal that would sensationally send the match to yet another penalty shoot-out.

With just one minute remaining, a high looping ball was sent into the River penalty area. Substitute Tiago Luis leaped and glanced the ball downwards and towards goal. The ball bounced past the stranded goalkeeper and looked like it would nestle in the top of the target. But it continued to rise agonisingly and ricocheted off the crossbar. The Big Green players dropped to their knees in unison.

And so it ended. Chape were eliminated, but in the most heroic way possible: they had beaten one of the very top teams in South America. Not just their own families and supporters, but the whole of the country, were proud of Associação Chapecoense de Futebol. It was an historic evening for the *Clube de Futebol*.

The fantastic performances and results continued in the *Brasileiro* as Chape defeated Fluminense and, once again, Internacional to mathematically confirm they had survived in *Série A* yet again and had done so with three matches to spare.

A 14th-place finish in the top division of the *Brasileiro* meant an improvement in their final position for the seventh consecutive campaign since narrowly qualifying for *Série D* via a second-place finish in the 2009 *Campeonato Catarinense*. How could they possibly continue their miraculous rise for an eighth season?

There would be a third consecutive *Série A* campaign for the veterans such as Neném, Nivaldo and Bruno Rangel. Danilo was forging a reputation as a top-class *goleiro*. These athletes had dragged themselves and their families to a quality of life they had previously only dreamed of.

Chape would resume their love affair with the *Copa Sul Americana* in 2016 following another qualification.

Immediately following the final game of the season, President Pallaoro, Vice-President Mauro Stumpf and long-serving football director and guru Cadu Gaúcho began planning for 2016, with emphasis on making a strong start; they desperately wanted to win their first *Campeonato Catarinense* in five years.

14

Pentacampeonato II

Ten years earlier, only the most hardened and stubborn of supporters were still in love with Associação Chapecoense de Futebol. During the stale and debt-ridden decades, young generations of soccer fans were looking further afield for the club whose flag they would fly for all of their lives; they would look into the neighbouring states and choose to support Grêmio, or Internacional et cetera. Attendances at the Arena Condá were recorded in three figures, rather than four.

But this decade had been different. Year on year the team had improved its standing within the *Brasileiro* and the support base had returned. The men, women and children of Chapecó now had their *Clube de Futebol* deep within their hearts. In almost every conversation in the friendly hometown community, the opening sentences would be of Chape; of their latest win, of their next exciting fixture, of the newest star added to the ranks, of Bruno Rangel and Marcos Danilo Padilha. Attendances at the Arena Condá were recorded in five figures, rather than four.

The family feel of the club brought the best performances out of everyone from President Pallaoro down to the laundry ladies.

Journeymen professionals such as Neném, Nivaldo, Danilo and Rangel, had seemed destined to end their careers like the millions that had preceded them: having never made it to the big leagues, living close to the poverty line and being forced into manual labour to support their families when their bodies would no longer allow them to play professional soccer. Now they were wealthy local heroes making national headlines.

It was felt they needed to add some silverware to the achievements of this golden generation; Guto Ferreira and his troops were instructed to go out and win the state championship for the first time in five years.

The 2016 *Campeonato Catarinense* took another obscure format: ten teams would play one another once in Phase One, then all reset to zero points and play the reverse set of fixtures in Phase Two. The winners of the two separate leagues would then progress to the two-legged final. If the same team won both, they would be the champions.

Chape won the first league stage with ease. They were victorious in seven and drew two of the nine matches to guarantee themselves a place in the final at the very least.

On 20 March, old rivals Avaí visited the Arena Condá for a match in the second league stage. Bruno Rangel had been back amongst the goals and found himself on a total of 62 scored for the Big Green going into the game, level with the legendary Índio, who had held the goalscoring record for the club for over 40 years.

With 20 minutes of the match gone, *capitão* Cléber Santana stood over a free kick in a dangerous position. With attackers and defenders alike awaiting the delivery, Santana typically floated the ball in perfectly. With his back to goal, stood on the penalty spot, Rangel used his strength to hold off the defenders, his vision to spot the opportunity and his finesse to gently caress the ball goalwards. It caught the *goleiro* unawares and he was helpless to stop it finding the bottom corner of the net.

Rangel performed his customary celebration, pointing skywards as his friends mobbed him, safe in the knowledge he had further increased his legend in Chapecó: he was now their greatest ever *atacante*.

By half-time it was three goals to nil. Bruno had scored a hat-trick. All three goals showed the subtle finishing of a man who simply knew he would score and shared an uncanny resemblance to his hero Romario. His cool and calm demeanour was not shared by his family, his team-mates or his supporters, who were delirious with joy. He had come back from a period in which it looked as though his career was over and his glorious *Série B* campaign was the finest he could ever manage, to once again become the goalscoring hero for Chapecoense and a proven *Série A atacante*.

It had looked possible, with three games remaining, that Chape may win the second stage too. They were a goal up, thanks once again to Rangel, against Metropolitano, of *Série D*, but the lowly side rallied and scored two late goals to cause an upset and derail the charge of the Big Green. This was largely down to an outstanding performance by a 22-year-old *atacante* by the name of Tiago. Cadu Gaúcho and Mauro Stumpf watched his performance with great interest.

Subsequently, Chape could not stop their other old adversaries Joinville winning the second league stage to set up a mouth-watering and nostalgic two-legged final that brought back memories of the controversy of 1996.

Due to their advancing years Neném and Rangel were used sparingly. The tactics of *técnico* Ferreira for the specific games would dicate who got the main *atacante* role. Rangel was sharing this position with young attacking midfielder Ananias. For both games that would make up the final, youth would get the nod over experience as Rangel took a seat on the substitutes' bench. Danilo and captain Cléber Santana would be included in a seemingly strong Chape team.

The first leg, on 1 May, would be at the Arena Joinville and Chape won by a fantastic and powerful late headed goal from Ananias. The players and supporters celebrated the goal as if it had already won them the championship, so confident were they in their form at the Arena Condá.

One week later, naturally and favourably for Chape, it was a day of torrential rain. Every running step of the players and every bounce of the ball brought a huge splash of water from the turf. The water would stop passes reaching their intended targets and slide-tackling defenders were unable to stop until they struck the advertising boards.

Just minutes before half-time, a Joinville corner kick was swung into the penalty area and a lapse in concentration allowed them to head the ball past Danilo and cancel out the Chape lead.

The victory so desperately wanted and expected by Chape was now in immense doubt.

In the second half, the rain-soaked pitch worsened. This, combined with the tension-ridden players, made for a seemingly amateur standard of match as no team could put a passage of play together. If it had not been for the already too relentless schedule of the Brazilian football calendar, the referee would surely have deemed the game unplayable.

With 30 minutes of play remaining, Guto Ferreira put on the talismanic Bruno Rangel. Just five minutes later, new Chape star Lucas Gomes, a Fluminense reject, slid a pass through the Joinville defence for Rangel. As the ball ran further to the left of the goal, the angle widened as did the chances of Bruno scoring. But, as always, the calmest man of the near 20,000 inside the stadium was the Chapecoense legend. As the defenders and goalkeeper closed upon him, he dragged the ball inside the penalty area, before analysing the tiny space between the opposition players through which he had to aim. He calmly swept the ball along the line which he had measured and into the net, initiating delirium inside the stadium as he slid along the sodden turf pointing his fingers skywards.

The supporters were wearing the familiar clear plastic raincoats that should accompany the purchase of any Chapecoense match ticket as the referee blew for full time and a pitch invasion from every member of the Chape family began.

Traditionally, at the trophy-giving ceremony of a football final, the captain of the victorious team lifts the trophy first. But with a team as closely knit as this, no single individual could have the honour. So current *capitão* Cléber Santana called former skippers and club legends Nivaldo, Rafael Lima and Neném to gather around the trophy, and they all lifted it together as fireworks, cheers and songs erupted into the now clear night sky.

Like their national team heroes, Associação Chapecoense de Futebol had achieved their own *Pentacampeonato* as they won their fifth state championship title.

Despite their *Deus*-like status in the city, the players were part of the community. Every day they would stop in the streets to chat to supporters about the next match, or the one that had just taken place. Or just about the rainy weather. They would visit children's hospitals and be guests of honour at charity functions.

Danilo, other than during matches and at training, was always seen with his toddler son, Lorenzo. They were inseparable. Crowds would form around the penalty area at the Arena Condá as, on the rare sunny days, Danilo began to teach his two-year-old son after training how to be a *goleiro*.

15

Corinthians Paulista

During the mid to late 19th century, the sport of association football was in its infancy, and almost unrecognisable from the global game we know today. It was still an amateur sport and was not played with tactics and finesse, but with the brutal force of large men simply chasing down a heavy leather ball and clattering into each other.

Whilst popular in Great Britain, it had barely been exported beyond those shores, and had zero exposure at all outside of Europe.

International football was solely played between the British teams, with Scotland the dominant nation. They would play against England in March, annually, a tradition that began in 1872. Scotland won seven of the first 11 contests, usually by high scorelines. Assistant secretary of the English Football Association N. Lane Jackson decided to take action. He wanted the best young amateur players from the southern districts of the country to play and practise together on a weekly basis.

In September 1882, Corinthian Football Club was born. The players were the greatest athletes from the best private universities. They trained together and devised tactics, formations and passing drills. They played in white cotton collared shirts. They were gentlemen and scholars as well as the finest athletes in the country.

'The Corinthians' soon made up almost all of the England team and on two occasions, both against Wales, the whole starting 11 was from the club.

In the 1888 edition of the 'Battle of Britain', England destroyed Scotland by five goals to nil, and began to dominate their rivals from that point onwards. The vision of Mr Jackson had come to fruition.

Corinthian FC continued to go from strength to strength and soon became national heroes. Too good to compete at the amateur club level, they began exhibition tours as tens of thousands would fill stadia around the country to capacity to be thrilled and entertained.

Meanwhile, 5,000 miles away in Brazil, Englishmen and Scotsmen were working together as engineers, building the first major railway system in South America. John Miller, a Scottish engineer, had lived in São Paulo for many years when his Brazilian wife of English descent gave birth to a son, Charles, in 1874. At the age of 10, Charles was sent to England for private schooling in Southampton. He discovered and fell in love with the beautiful game, and became an excellent player in his teenage years.

The Corinthians were to complete their 1892 tour against Hampshire County in Southampton and the local sports fans and schools clambered into the stadium to watch the match. Due to the long and arduous tour, Corinthian arrived with only ten fit players. The teacher of Charles Miller volunteered his precocious young talent to pull on the mythical white shirt and play with the god-like, moustachioed stars. The 17-year-old excelled on the left wing and did not look out of place in the greatest team in the land.

In a repeat of the same tie in March 1894, Miller was now representing his county and so played against his heroes. After he starred again in the tie, the players and representatives of the Corinthians approached him about his future, but he explained that, at just 19, he had just played his final football match. With his education complete, he was about to head for the epic boat journey back to Brazil, where he would join his father in engineering the railways. Football was not even a thought where he would be going.

The Corinthians wished him well on his travels and gave him the gift of two iconic, signed footballs to take with him. He also took a copy of the official Association Football Rulebook.

When the young Miller finally landed back in São Paulo and began work, he took the footballs with him. During breaks from the exhausting work, he would teach the local, poverty-stricken labourers the sport. Filled with joy, they would subsequently go home and play with their children and friends, using rolled up clothes and papers as a ball.

Charles then introduced the game to Clube Atlético São Paulo, a sports club from which the railway workers had played cricket. A *futebol* team was formed. Like a forest fire through the Amazon, over the months and years to come the sport spread, with new teams and pitches being set up, so it became a national pastime.

Miller was then instrumental in organising the inaugural *Campeonato Paulista:* the first ever edition of the first state championship, which took place in 1902 and has been run every single year since. Clube Atlético São Paulo won each of the opening three *Campeonato Paulistas,* with Charles Miller the top goalscorer in two of the campaigns. Other states soon had their own championships, and instigated the thrilling league format on which the *Brasileiro* is now built.

Meanwhile, the Corinthians' tours had gone international, as they attempted to make 'the Beautiful Game' they had devised global. Starting in 1897, they completed a total of nine overseas tours in Europe, South Africa and North America. Their tenth tour took place in 1910 and brought them to Brazil, where the game had now grown into a national obsession.

When he heard of the scheduled tour, Charles Miller made contact with representatives of Corinthian, who remembered him well and fondly. They prepared the tour in such a way that it would culminate against Clube Atlético São Paulo, and Miller, 18 years after playing for them, would once again play against the legendary squad.

The Corinthians had scored 30 goals in the first five games of the Brazilian tour and were evolving the sport to new levels, with passing and dribbling manoeuvres the likes of which had never been seen before. All of the local railway workers packed into the stadium to see their friend and colleague represent their city against the immortal Englishmen.

Sensationally, Charles Miller, at the age of 36, scored against the Corinthians in an 8–2 defeat that thrilled the fanatical but impoverished natives. On 4 September 1910, *O Jogo Bonito* and the Brazilian thirst for a swashbuckling and electrifying brand of soccer was born.

All the *clubes de futebol* that had been formed in Brazil were founded by the upper classes, and the sport was seen as one played by the rich and only watched by the poor. But five of the railway workers who knew Miller were so inspired by what they had seen, they set up a new team to represent the lower, working classes of São Paulo.

On 10 September 1910, *Sport Club Corinthians Paulista* played their first match, in a friendly against an established amateur side. They lost by just one goal, but the tens of thousands of local poverty-battling football obsessives had begun to see them as the side that represented them. So they trained hard to improve their own skills and clamoured and competed to play for them.

In 1913, Corinthians Paulista played in the *Campeonato Paulista* for the first time. Just the following year, they won it for the first time.

Now, with 24 million supporters, 28 state championship titles, seven *Série A* championships and two FIFA Club World Cups, Corinthians Paulista are one of the most historic and celebrated football clubs on the planet.

Charles Miller lived his whole life in São Paulo, and continued to play cricket and golf there in his later years. He is also credited with increasing the popularity of those sports in Brazil, but is most fondly remembered as their 'Father of Football'. He died in the city aged 78 in 1953. Five years and one day later, Brazil and 17-year-old Pelé won the *Copa do Mundo* for the first time.

Back in England, as the game became ultra-professional, the Corinthians could no longer attract the best stars. But they insisted they would forever remain an amateur club, and to this day they are the highest placed non-professional football club in the enormous pyramid structure of the country. Their current guise is Corinthian-Casuals, following a merger with a neighbouring side.

The 2015 *Brasileiro Série A* was won quite easily by Corinthians Paulista. They had been so good that when, in the spring of 2016, the Brazilian national team required yet another new *técnico*, they headhunted the man behind the Corinthians glory: the very popular 55-year-old Adenor Leonardo Bacchi; commonly known as Tite (pronounced Tee-Tay).

His remit was to take the *Canarinhos* to the 2018 World Cup in Russia and reinvigorate a team that were possibly at their lowest ever point. The supporters needed to feel pride in the iconic yellow jersey once again.

Chapecoense fitness coach Anderson Paixão, had gained such a reputation from the fact that so many seemingly average players in the Big Green shirt raised their games and got every ounce of performance from their limited ability, that the Brazilian Football Confederation contacted him and offered him a part-time role with the *Canarinhos*. It was a dream come true for him. His father, Paulo, had been the Brazilian team fitness coach for the 2002 *Copa do Mundo* glory and was the hero of Anderson, who now had the opportunity to emulate him at the 2018 tournament.

16

Amado

Ahead of another relentless campaign of up to 60 *Série A*, *Copa do Brasil* and *Copa Sul Americana* matches in the next eight months, President Pallaoro, Cadu Gaúcho and Mauro Stumpf added to the Chape squad once again. As usual, the budget was tiny. So, in came players with the usual profile: young and hungry with something to prove, and good people that would fit in well with the Chapecoense family.

Silvio, who had disappointed in goal when called upon and lasted less than half a game before the Eternal had to come to his rescue, had left the club. He was replaced by Jakson Follmann, a 24-year-old *goleiro* who had been an understudy at Grêmio before being released. He had since spent the latest two campaigns with clubs competing only in state championships. He would now be the first-choice replacement for Danilo, with Nivaldo, now 42, the emergency back-up.

There was also a returning face in that of Alan Ruschel, who had spent two seasons as reserve left-back for Internacional, but would now return to the Arena Condá on loan. He had been a hugely popular figure during his first spell at the club and would be another great addition to the unique family atmosphere that surrounded the changing room and the entire club.

They also brought in the youngster that had terrorised their defence in the state championship match against lowly

Metropolitano. The overjoyed and enthusiastic Tiago moved to Chapecó with young wife Graziele for the life-changing opportunity. The pair were utterly besotted with one another, and Cadu Gaúcho saw the 21-year-old as the eventual replacement for Bruno Rangel. But he was a very raw talent: electrifyingly quick, but seemed rash on the ball, almost overly enthusiastic. He was also very slender, and would need strengthening up, if he was to be the new Bruno.

Now they were established within *Série A*, Chape's top performers were earning as much as $30,000 per month. Danilo was always the picture of happiness. Chatty and polite, as a term of endearment he would call his friends and team-mates *'amado'*, and the women in his life *'amada'*, which translate as 'beloved'. He sensibly invested almost all of his hefty salary into local properties and didn't have the fancy cars and watches that many of his friends began treating themselves to. He would say that his goal was to create a good life for his *amada* wife Letícia and his *amado* son Lorenzo.

Following the *Campeonato Catarinense* glory, the confidence and vibrancy of Chapecoense was at an all-time high as the *Série A* season got underway. The good results, particularly at the cauldron that was the Arena Condá, continued as Chape proved they were an established top-tier *Brasileiro* team. They were hovering around the middle of the table with no real fears of another relegation struggle. Guto Ferreira was utilising his new, bigger squad. Tiago was making *Série A* appearances from the substitutes' bench, as was Bruno Rangel, in a bid to keep him at optimum fitness levels for the crucial time when his team would desperately need his goal instinct.

After the opening ten rounds of matches, with Chape sitting comfortably in 12th position in the standings, Guto Ferreira shocked them by ending his very successful ten-month tenure to surprisingly take over as *técnico* at *Série B* side Bahia. This was, however, a blessing in disguise for the management team as they saw an opportunity to get in a coach they had sought after for many years in Luiz Carlos Salori. Known as Caio Júnior, the 51-year-old *técnico* had over 15 years' experience in the *Brasileiro* and had coached the likes of Palmeiras, Flamengo and Grêmio.

President Pallaoro and his management team had wanted him for the previous two vacancies but he had been under contract elsewhere. He had most recently been coaching in the United Arab Emirates but had returned to Brazil and was actively seeking a role in *Série A*.

Almost immediately following the exit of Ferreira, Caio Júnior arrived at the Arena Condá. He was so enamoured by the club, their progress and the project, that he didn't even discuss the salary on offer before agreeing to take on the role.

Caio Júnior settled into the club immediately and felt at ease with the playing squad and the management, singling out President Pallaoro and director Jandir Bordignon for praise regarding the friendly welcome that helped him settle so quickly.

If it was possible to improve on the changing room and training ground harmony that had previously been instilled at Chape, Caio Júnior achieved it.

At the end of August, the *Copa Sul Americana* adventure restarted once again. With 32 of the greatest teams in South America left in the tournament, Chapecoense would begin their 2016 journey with a seemingly simple tie against a fellow *Brasileiro* team: Cuiabá of northern State Mato Grosso.

Cuiabá were a *Série C* outfit that had managed to qualify for the *Sul Americana* by surprisingly winning the 2015 *Copa Verde*: a knockout tournament of lower-ranked teams from the north of Brazil.

Thus, Caio Júnior decided to save some of his star players for the more difficult challenges ahead and put out a team of mostly second-choice players for the first leg of the tie, away in Mato Grosso.

The decision backfired as the underdogs found an inner belief and strength to defeat Chape 1–0 in a manner that resembled the overachieving heroics of the Big Green themselves over the previous decade.

In the return leg, many first-choice performers returned to the fray, as did the torrential Chapecó rain. Optimism was high that the star players so used to the wet conditions under the bright lights of the Arena Condá would comfortably turn around the one-goal deficit. But after 22 minutes, a corner kick was swung in by Cuiabá and a lapse in concentration by the defenders led to a clear headed opportunity, which found the bottom corner of Danilo's netting. Disaster. An away goal. Chapecoense now had to score three.

At half-time, President Sandro Pallaoro himself left his seat in the stadium and charged to the Chapecoense changing room to remind them what they were about to lose, and what they had to gain. He told them he believed they could, and would, turn the match around in the remaining 45 minutes.

Half of that time disappeared without meaningful event and the Chape supporters were growing disgruntled as they once again stood in their clear plastic raincoats on a sad and wet Chapecó evening. Suddenly, there was hope. A dangerous free kick led to a melee in the Cuiabá penalty area, and Chape winger Lucas Gomes managed to squeeze the ball into the goal.

Just two minutes later, another Chape attack saw a shot go past the diving Cuiabá *goleiro*, only to strike the inside of the post and agonisingly cross the goalmouth before hitting the other stanchion too and ricocheting away towards the corner flag. But quickest to react to the pandemonium was Rangel, who sprinted to halt the ball from getting too far away from danger. His momentum on the sodden grass looked certain to take him into the stands but he managed to stop himself, pivot and turn back to the ball that he had made stationary. With defenders uncontrollably sprinting and sliding toward him and the forlorn goalkeeper still down on the grass from the initial save, Bruno instinctively wrapped his extraordinary right foot around the ball, raised it over his grounded foes and curled it into the goal from the most impossible of angles. Sensing a sensational comeback, he followed the ball into the goal and collected it, sprinting to the centre of the pitch to hurry a restart.

The tie was locked at two goals each but Chape needed to hit the back of the net one more time with 20 minutes remaining to overcome the away goals rule.

Like so many times over the previous few years, the tension inside the Arena Condá was palpable as Chape launched attack after attack. With just eight minutes left on the clock, *capitão* Cléber Santana sent the ball wide to the left where his comrade wasted no time in swinging it into a dangerous position towards the near post of the goal, seeking out Lucas Gomes. Gomes leapt with all his might but the ball was slightly too high and merely brushed the top of his head, deflecting it back toward the penalty spot at high pace. There stood the incomparable Bruno Rangel, who adjusted his position to the new path of the ball in the blink of an eye, before controlling it beautifully on his left thigh and thrashing it into the goal with the foot of the same leg without the ball touching the floor.

Like he had so many times before, Bruno made the Arena Condá erupt with wild celebrations. The dream would not be ending so prematurely. The adventure, the journey, would continue. In the next round a few weeks later, Chape would play Argentinian giants Independiente in the last 16 of the tournament.

For *Brasileiro* matches, as many as 12 substitutes can be named, even though only three can be used. Effectively, coaches in *Série A* can name all of their fit and available players as substitutes to give themselves maximum choices to change their on-field team, dependent on the infinite possibilities of things that may happen in the 90 minutes of adrenaline-charged action. Often, even multiple substitute goalkeepers are named, despite even one only being required on the rarest of occasions.

In CONMEBOL competitions, the registered number of players is smaller and only seven substitutes can be named for match days. Therefore, it had been decided that Nivaldo, given his extremely advancing years, would not be in the *Copa Sul Americana* squad. Jakson Follmann would be the substitute *goleiro* to provide cover for Danilo.

With his team comfortably sat in a mid-table position in *Série A*, Caio Júnior decided to play some of his usual substitutes from the start in the match before the *Copa Sul Americana* tie. This included young Tiago, who had impressed everyone at the club with not only his football skills, but also his work ethic and enthusiasm.

The game was a home tie against Ponte Preta. With little over ten minutes of the match gone, Tiago broke into the penalty area and brilliantly cut inside, sending his defender skidding out of play on the – as always – soaking wet ground. It was now a race to the ball between Tiago and the goalkeeper. The fleet-footed youngster narrowly made it there first, before showing the calmness of a veteran to gently flick the ball over the advancing *goleiro* and into the goal. He dropped to his knees and wept as his new friends rushed to join him in celebration. He was now not only a *Série A* player, but a *Série A* goalscorer. As he got to his feet, he pointed to his *amada* wife Graziele as she watched on in joy from the stands alongside the other wives of the Chape family.

In the second half, central defender Filipe Machado – also a new signing and someone who, at the age of 32, had never made it above *Série B* in the *Brasileiro* before the legendary Chapecoense talent scouts saw something within him – saw Tiago making a run through the defensive line of Ponte Preta. Machado exquisitely launched a pass the whole length of the field. Tiago brilliantly controlled the ball as it fell from the sky, before dispatching it into the net for his second goal. So impressive had Tiago been, it was clear he would no longer be starting even the most important of matches alongside the substitutes.

For the first leg against Independiente, Chape made the 800-mile journey to the town of Avallaneda near to Buenos Aires. They were going there with the usual target in mind: try to hold their technically superior opponents to a 0–0 draw and bring them back to the fortress of the Arena Condá, where the vociferous and passionate support acted as a 12th man on the pitch, and the weather could act as a 13th.

That mission of a goalless first leg was accomplished.

One week later, under the floodlights at the Arena Condá, the stalemate continued until the referee blew his whistle and sparked the unbearable tension that only a penalty shoot-out to decide such an important match can create.

Alternate penalty kicks would be taken, Chape going first, with the team that scored the most out of the five selected kickers progressing in the tournament.

Big Green defender Thiego stepped up first as the crowd took their first giant breath, unsure whether the exhale would be a shallow sigh taken alongside the sinking of the shoulders and chest, or an ecstatic cheer as fists punched the air.

Unfortunately, it was the former as Thiego struck the crossbar. Advantage Independiente.

Next, Argentinian striker Benítez would go face to face with Danilo. As the ball was struck, Danilo dived to his right. He judged correctly. He successfully saved before bouncing back to his feet and joining his flock in a fierce outpouring of energy.

All square.

Capitão Cléber Santana then made the walk from the middle of the field where his team-mates were looking on nervously, with arms around one another's shoulders. He confidently attempted to pass the ball straight down the middle, assuming the goalkeeper would dive one way or the other. But he didn't. Instead, he stood stationary to simply parry the ball away from the goal.

Advantage Independiente.

Striker Vera smashed the ball beyond Danilo to confirm the lead of his team.

To the relief of everyone, after almost four hours of play against this foe, Chape finally found the net as Filipe Machado confidently struck the ball into the bottom corner of the goal.

Midfielder Emiliano Rigoni looked to regain the vital advantage for his team as he began to run toward the ball. He struck it firmly to the right of Danilo, who displayed more cat-like reactions to get down low and block the ball and once again launch into wild celebrations with 20,000 delighted fans.

All square.

The next penalty for each team was scored to maintain the deadlock going into the final scheduled round of kicks. Caio Júnior had saved his most reliable taker, Bruno Rangel, for the most pressurised kick.

Like he was taking a practice penalty, Rangel calmly brushed the ball safely into the corner of the goal before jogging over to his friend Danilo to wish him luck. Danilo was unable to stop the shoot-out being taken to an even further level of tension: sudden death.

Caio Júnior sat in his dugout, with his head in his hands. He couldn't watch.

Agonisingly, the next penalty of Chape was missed to send the Arena into despair. If Sanchez Minõ scored, and at this level approximately 75 per cent of penalties are successful, the journey would be over for another year.

Danilo played mind games with him. He had already faced six penalty kicks and had dived right for most, making two saves when doing so. Minõ took the gamble that Danilo would finally change his tactic as he struck the ball low to the right of the inspired *goleiro*. Danilo did not change his tactic. He once again dived swiftly to his right to repel the ball away from the goal line. The celebration was even more wild than before.

All square.

The pressure was becoming intolerable as another successful kick was taken for each team to take the shoot-out to a third sudden-death round.

Up stepped young Tiago. Left-footed, he struck the ball high. The despairing goalkeeper got his raised hand to the ball but was unable to take enough momentum from it to prevent it bouncing over the line. Finally, it was advantage Chapecoense.

Danilo resumed the nocturnal prowl back to his goal line, staring at the advancing next kicker, stalking his prey.

Independiente had finally had to resort to one of their less confident defenders to take a kick. The nervous Tagliafico seemed rushed as he quickly ran towards the ball. Amazingly, he went to the right of Danilo, who was still not changing his tactic. Powerfully outstretched, he reached the ball with both hands to deflect it far from goal and spark yet more scenes of jubilation.

His team-mates that had stood and watched his dynamic display sprinted with all their might towards their hero. He had played almost four hours of *futebol* against one of the top teams of Argentina without conceding a goal, and had subsequently saved four penalties in the shoot-out decider to send his team into the quarter-final of the *Copa Sul Americana* once again.

This Chapecoense team shared so much with the 1994 World Cup winning legends which inspired them; not only did they use *Era Parreira* tactics, but their two star players were their white, charismatic *goleiro* and their black, calm, clinical *atacante*.

Marcos Danilo Padilha had joined Bruno Rangel in the annals of immortality in the city of Chapecó.

They were beloved. They were *amado*.

17

LaMia

Just eight years earlier, Chapecoense had been playing solely in competitions that meant they would never have to travel outside their own state of Santa Catarina. They had since been on many epic journeys and adventures, but the quarter-final of the 2016 *Copa Sul Americana* would take them the greatest distance possible from Chapecó in a South American competition.

They were to play Atlético Junior, from the city of Barranquilla, in the north-western point of Colombia, approximately 4,000 miles from Chapecó.

Given the large-scale party required to travel for the highly anticipated encounter, including journalists and club officials, the decision was taken by the Chapecoense management that, for the first time, they would charter their own dedicated flight. The new Bolivian airline of *LaMia* was hired, having only opened for business in January 2016.

LaMia had originally been started as a Venezuelan airline in 2009, with a fleet of three RJ85 aeroplanes. But after repeatedly failing to get operations started due to permit, licensing and certification problems, in 2015 they decided to lease the fleet of aircraft to a trio of Bolivian entrepreneurs looking to start their own charter airline, which would specialise in corporate travel for large businesses, with football clubs and international teams seen as the perfect clientele.

The entrepreneurs were businessman Gustavo Vargas Gamboa as well as experienced pilots Marco Antonio Rocha and Miguel Quiroga. They opted to retain the name *LaMia* in a cost-cutting exercise as the branding and signage was then already on their fleet. As the new company opened for business, Rocha and Quiroga were named as co-owners with Gamboa in the position of CEO.

The business model was working. They had flown multiple football clubs around South America as well as the national teams of Venezuela, Bolivia and even the superstar-laden team of Argentina, including Lionel Messi.

For Chapecoense, the initial idea was to charter one flight from São Paulo direct to Barranquilla. But as the itinerary was drawn up, it emerged *LaMia* did not have the authority to fly in Brazilian airspace and so it was arranged that the Chape party would instead get a commercial flight to the northern city of Cuiabá, where they had played their first game of the tournament. From there they would get a bus over the Bolivian border to meet the *LaMia* aircraft and crew and complete their journey to Colombia.

The journey went smoothly and comfortably and was seen as a new adventure for everyone involved, one they enjoyed. The return journey went similarly well, also carried out in the disjointed manner which enabled the aviation rules to be adhered to. Unfortunately, Chape had lost the match in Colombia 1–0 so would once again face elimination unless they could overturn the deficit at the Arena Condá.

Seven days later, the big match atmosphere came back to Chapecó, as did the relentless rains. The 20,000 plastic overcoats accompanied the tension and excitement as the Big Green attempted to go one better in the 2016 adventure than they had exactly one year earlier.

If Atlético Junior hadn't travelled 4,000 miles for the occasion, the referee may well have postponed the encounter, so horrendous was the weather. Every step of a player and bounce of the ball caused a hip-height release of water from the saturated turf. As always, these conditions favoured the Chapecoense stars as they were so experienced in them.

Knowing his team needed goals, Caio Júnior once again deployed his newly favoured team of *atacantes*, with Bruno Rangel flanked by the dynamic youngsters Ananias and Tiago. There was wave after wave of Chape pressure, but the chances created went begging; that was until Bruno Rangel drove the ball left-footed across the face of the goal, where his partner Ananias reacted quickest to fire the ball home, to the huge relief of the sodden supporters. The moment the ball hit the back of the net, Danilo, standing 40 yards from his goal line, such had been the siege at the opposite end of the pitch, turned and sprinted towards the fans, sliding on his knees in the swamp-like conditions, causing a continuous wave of liquid as he skated along for yard after yard.

By half-time, it was 2–0 and, with the rainwater dripping from their faces, the Júnior players were beaten. The game finished 3–0 to spark more scenes of immense celebration as thousands of supporters joined their idols on the field of play, and pandemonium ensued as the joyous masses slid and splashed inside the reservoir-like stadium. Associação Chapecoense de Futebol looked certain to finish in their best *Série A* position yet, and had now also added more to their history, as their greatest ever team would now compete in the semi-finals of the *Copa Sul Americana* in another huge Brazil versus Argentina clash, as they would once again make the relatively short trip to Buenos Aires to play the gigantic San Lorenzo.

San Lorenzo are the team supported by Pope Francis. They are 15 times champions of Argentina. Even by their historical high standards, this particular era was proving to be one of their most successful ever. Having won their national championship in 2013, they had gone on to win, in 2014, the *Copa Libertadores*; the South American version of the European Champions League.

Almost all of their squad was made up of international players who regularly represented the likes of Paraguay, Uruguay and even Argentina themselves. They had many players who had previously made the successful footballing pilgrimage to Europe and spent years in the top leagues in the world before returning to complete their glittering careers back in Bueno Aires. One of them was Fabricio Colloccini, who had spent a total of 17 years playing in the Italian, Spanish and English top divisions, including almost a decade as captain of Newcastle United, and had made 39 international appearances for Argentina.

Chapecoense had never had an internationally capped player in their ranks.

As was becoming inevitable on their extraordinary run in the competition, Chape would once again be on the road in the first leg. But in a change of tactics by Caio Júnior, so devastating had the attacking trio been against Atlético Junior, that he opted to start them in an unusually adventurous formation for the away leg of such a tie. The tactic that had worked so well to this point was to limit the damage as much as possible at the home of the opposition and then use the unique home advantages of the astronomical support of the fanatical fans and torrential micro-climate only Chapecó can create to beat their opposition into submission in the return game. His theory this time, was that with those three in such good form, Chape may well be able to snatch a crucial away goal.

On 2 November, the Big Green stars walked out into the 47,000-capacity Estádio Pedro Bidegain in the most important match of their careers. After a tentative start by both teams, which is expected in a match of this magnitude, San Lorenzo were awarded a dangerous free kick on the left side of the pitch. As you would expect from players of this calibre, the ball was swung into the penalty area with pace and precision. San Lorenzo defender Angeleri got ahead of his marker and looked set to head the ball back across Danilo, who instinctively moved to save what seemed to be the inevitable play. But Angeleri misjudged his leap and missed the ball completely. The wrong-footed *goleiro* was helplessly stranded as the ball agonisingly bounced into the far side of the goal to put Chapecoense one behind just 30 minutes into the total three-hour tie.

San Lorenzo were the better team by a considerable margin and it looked inevitable their lead would be doubled shortly as they pressured the Chape defence and created many good chances. But once again the Big Green could rely on an inspired Danilo to repel all that came his way.

A couple of dangerous counter-attacks buoyed Chape and reminded San Lorenzo that they were against a talented team with an inner strength. As the game progressed, Chape began to believe the away goal they had come in search of may well be possible.

Mid-way through the second half, another counter-attack led to Ananias holding the ball on the edge of the penalty area, with his back to goal and two defenders breathing down his neck. Scared to foul him and give away a penalty, the defenders simply held him in position as he seemingly posed no danger to their goal. Suddenly, the 27-year-old *atacante* spun through 180 degrees and simultaneously lashed the ball towards goal with his left foot. It flew between the defenders, who had unsighted the goalkeeper, who dived too late and despite getting his hand to the ball, was unable to stop it crossing the line. The Chape stars and coaches launched into celebratory hugs, as did the hundreds of loyal supporters that had made the long journey for the late Wednesday evening match.

Almost immediately, having achieved his target of scoring an away goal, Caio Júnior made changes to the tactics as his team now had the aggregate lead. Back came the *Era Parreira* style as the players wearing the green and white kit came closer together to guard the goal of Danilo at all costs. It worked. The game finished as a 1–1 draw and so rather than having to overturn a deficit at the Arena Condá as they had usually had to, they now had an away goal lead to defend.

Excruciatingly for all associated with the club, there was a three-week gap between the two legs of the tie. Meanwhile, the overachieving, closely bonded team of youngsters, veterans, rejects and journeymen had been in staggeringly good form in *Série A*. On 20 November they comfortably beat the giants of São Paulo by two goals to nil, the jubilant and vibrant Tiago again on the scoresheet. Amazingly, the result put Chapecoense in eighth position in the standings, above the established and historic clubs Internacional, Cruzeiro, Fluminense, defending champions Corinthians Paulista and latest victims São Paulo themselves.

The whole of Brazil became green and white. The *Esporte* pages of the media were awash with support for Chapecoense as they prepared to go head to head in a classical Argentina versus Brazil, winner-takes-all showdown. The exciting and familiar mid-week routine resumed once again. The team would all stay at the Hotel Bertaso the evening before the colossal match to gain maximum rest and the best possible preparation. The hotel had released the whole of the second floor to them.

After settling into their room at the hotel, Tiago and his roommate were sitting on the floor in the hallway, relaxing together in their Chape training attire. They were approached by defender Caramelo and midfielder Matheus Biteco, who was carrying a white gift bag decorated with silver glitter. He handed it to Tiago.

Assuming it was some kind of prank, he took it hesitantly, gripping it far away from himself with the tip of his thumb and index finger, looking around suspiciously at the friends that surrounded him. They told him it was a present from a female admirer amongst the supportive crowd that had welcomed the team outside the hotel.

Tiago sighed and disdainfully threw the bag to one side. He told his friends he did not want to be seen to be encouraging this sort of behaviour, such was his love for his wife, Graziele.

Caramelo picked up the bag and insisted that opening the present is a show of gratitude to a supporter, and that to refuse it just based on the fact it was a girl would be rude. Tiago was still unsure. He opened the card first and his eyes immediately sank into a stare, frozen for a few seconds. He then quickly slammed it back shut, closed his eyes and took a deep breath before allowing himself to read the words once again. He reopened the card to confirm the words were still there, staring at them longer still this time around.

Suddenly he leapt to his feet and began to dance and cheer. His friends joined him in his moment of personal glory, sharing hugs and laughter. Tiago then lifted a pair of tiny shoes from the gift bag. It had all been a ruse orchestrated by Graziele, a dramatic way to surprise her husband with the fantastic news that he was going to be a daddy.

In yet another flashback to the 1994 World Cup, the joyous men began to do the imaginary baby-cradling goal celebration made famous by Bebeto when he scored in the *Copa do Mundo*. The dance has since become part of Brazilian football folklore and is always carried out when a goalscorer has recently become a father.

Tiago went on to spend the evening and the following day texting Graziele; they were even discussing baby names. Finally, his team-mates told him to put down his phone as it was time to leave the hotel for the gargantuan match. He sent one last text, telling Graziele he loved her.

As the darkness set over the city, all its residents made their way to the streets, waving their green and white flags. The black night was lit in the same familiar colour scheme as flares and fireworks were shot skywards. In unison, they endlessly sang the songs of support to their team of heroes, and it seemed that the whole city had joined in.

The sea of people had to part as the team bus arrived at the stadium, which was already full and acting as a volcano of noise as the same chants erupted from its open-air ceiling.

In the changing room, the 40-strong squad of players, coaches, staff and management linked arm in arm and took it in turns to convey their messages of confidence and support for each other.

Combined, the message was clear: do not leave that field with any regrets, play with your heart, play for the club, play for your families.

The instructions and tactics were just as transparent: stay close to each other to create a defensive unit so tight that the more talented players of San Lorenzo cannot breach the goal. If the target of a 0–0 draw could be accomplished, qualification for the final would be secured in the greatest night in the 43-year history of Associação Chapecoense de Futebol. This was about to be *Era Parreira* on steroids.

Chape defended, and defended well. Despite their technically superior foes having almost all of the possession, they limited their chances at goal to just a couple, which the trusty Danilo was more than equal to.

This match, with these tactics, was pure torture for everyone associated with the club and the city looking on. If they could have travelled through time, their destination would have been 10pm, when the torture would be over.

Half-time came and went, but the 45 minutes had felt like an eternity. The second half would feel even longer.

The hour mark of the match arrived, and the target scoreline was still intact. The Arena Condá and its loyal army of Chapecó disciples had gotten used to tense finales over this decade, but this was beyond what their human hearts could stand. The 90th minute arrived and the assistant referee held up the number four on his electronic board, signifying at least another 240 seconds of agony for the Chape supporters.

In over three hours of football against San Lorenzo, only one defensive mistake had been made, which led to the goal in Bueno Aires. That came from a free kick in a dangerous wide position. With 93 minutes and 30 seconds on the clock, Chape gave them an opportunity that was eerily similar. This would be the final play of the whole tie. It had all come down to this. Clear the ball without it entering the goal and Chapecoense would sensationally be in the final of the *Copa Sul Americana*. Fail to do so and the dream would be over.

The ball was delivered with predictable quality, and after a small scramble, it arrived at the feet of the same San Lorenzo defender, Angeleri, that had misjudged the headed chance which then wrong-footed Danilo for the previous goal. He was six yards out, bearing down on the centre of the net.

The crazed stadium fell silent. Both hands clasped every face in the Arena as the time that had been going so slowly now stopped altogether.

Angeleri struck the ball low and true. That was all that mattered from such a tiny distance, as no one could react quickly enough to stop it crashing into the goal. Twenty thousand hearts sank inside the stadium, and ten times more did so throughout the country. Except for, of course, Marcos Danilo Padilha, who instinctively pushed his right leg as far as it would stretch to deflect the ball away from the goal when it was just inches away from crossing the line. He jumped back to his feet and let out an almighty roar and pounded his chest with both gloved fists.

The stadium remained silent. The fans daren't believe the impossible save had just happened. Maybe the ball had crossed the line?

The quiet was finally broken from the commentary box. It was lifelong Chape supporter Rafael Henzel, who screamed at the top of his bellowing voice, *'Deus-nilo! Deus-nilo!'*. The commentator, sat alongside his friend and broadcast partner Renan Agnolin, vocally declared what everyone already knew: Marcos Danilo Padilha was *O Deus de Chapecó,* he was the God of Chapecó.

Born in 1973, the same year as Associação Chapecoense de Futebol, Rafael Henzel was a proud Chapecó resident. As a child, whilst Chape were scrapping away almost exclusively in the state championships, he would come to the games with no money and no ticket and stand outside the Arena Condá. Once the game got underway, he would find an unattended entrance and sneak in to see his Big Green heroes in action. He lived for Chapecoense. His adolescent skills, however, were clearly more academic than athletic and so he made the decision to train as a sports journalist, so that he could live as much of his life as possible in and around the *Clube de Futebol* that was at his heart.

Spending most of his 40 years around the lowly and unsuccessful team ensured Rafael grew into a pale, balding and chubby but always passionate reporter. He had been working as a commentator and journalist for the local media for many years and was a very popular part of the furniture around the Arena Condá. He hosted a local radio show alongside his broadcast and commentary partner, Renan Agnolin. He could never hide his bias and on the day they achieved promotion to the top division from *Série B,* he cried with joy into his live microphone.

Rafael was now shaking, sobbing and cheering with emotion once again and the crowd followed his lead and erupted deliriously as the referee put his whistle to his lips to signify the end; and the glory.

Danilo dropped to his knees, before sinking his head into his hands in a bid to contain his emotion.

For a decade Chapecoense had been advancing to the next stage in their progression by the narrowest of narrow margins. And they had done it again. That was why everyone loved Chape; it was always exciting.

Caio Júnior and all the players and staff rushed around in frenzied delirium. On the pitch, in the stands, in the changing room, across the city and the whole country, the celebrations lasted long into the night.

The team and their families went to a bar and restaurant to eat, relax and reflect on their achievement. The waiters were attentive to their guests of honour. Between them, the squad played a variety of musical instruments, which they did as the rest of the team sing along.

The wives and girlfriends were looking on proudly, but also revelling in their own joy at the announcement of the new pregnancy of Graziele.

18

Vôo 2933

Stuck on 299 Chapecoense appearances, the Eternal Nivaldo had been promised that he would start at least one of the two remaining *Série A* matches, to become the first player to make 300 Big Green appearances. He would then retire. He wasn't registered to play in the *Copa Sul Americana*. The final was once again over two matches, and naturally, the away leg came first. Like in the quarter-final, they would travel to Colombia, to go against Atlético Nacional, of Medellín, for the overall title.

The travel itinerary was discussed and the airline *LaMia* was hired once again for the final leg of the trip. On 26 November, the squad would fly from Chapecó to São Paulo where they would play Palmeiras the following day. They then wanted to charter a flight to go direct from São Paulo to Medellín on the Monday, but the application to the aviation authorities was refused once again due to *LaMia* not having the authority to fly in Brazil. So, it was decided instead they would get a commercial flight from São Paulo to Santa Cruz airport in Bolivia, where they would once again meet the *LaMia* flight crew, including its co-owner and pilot Miguel Quiroga, and fly with them to Medellín. They made the decision to change the flight plans rather than find a different charter airline company at this late stage. They had enjoyed the previous flight with *LaMia*, who showed a wonderful degree of customer service and made small gestures to make their guests feel special, such as hanging covers with the ACF club crest over the headrests of all of the seats. The company wanted to stand out and make a good impression on business travellers and football teams with this level of personalisalism.

The change to the initial plan meant fewer passengers were able to go, due to the late and mass booking of seats on the commercial flight. There were journalists, directors and staff in the party, and Caio Júnior was told he could take 22 players. With a heavy heart, he decided Nivaldo could not make the journey. He needed to give himself maximum options in his squad for the final, so only wanted to take two goalkeepers, and with Nivaldo not registered for the *Copa Sul Americana*, he would have to miss the whole trip. He would therefore get his 300th game in the very final match of the *Série A* campaign, an encounter with Atlético Mineiro following the return from Medellín. It also meant that he and Neném, who was still lacking fitness, would not travel for the away leg of the final

Always the gentlemen and loyal Chapecoense servants, the two club veteran legends told their *técnico* they understood, and he should not worry about the situation. They would support their team-mates from afar and welcome them back, and wait for the home tie to cheer on their beloved friends.

They were not the only Chapecoense legends to be missing the trip. Also invited were former influential board members Nei Maidana, *Conciliador* de Nes Filho and Maringá, who were still heavily involved with the club. Maidana was going to go, but his wife quickly pointed out that it clashed with a ballet recital that he had promised his four-year-old daughter he would be attending. Maidana tried to convince his wife that the Chape match was once in a lifetime, and he should be there. She countered by reminding him the second leg of the final would be in their hometown just one week later. They disagreed on the matter but when his child came to him in the evening, showing her daddy what she would be wearing at her ballet, he emotionally realised his wife was correct. He decided not to go on the five-day round trip.

Plínio David de Nes Filho was now 70 years old and had an important business meeting that clashed with the trip. He too decided to wait for the return leg of the final. Similarly, current Chapecó Mayor Luciano Buligon, whose association with the club also stretched back decades, disappointingly had to give up his seat on the plane due to political appointments in São Paulo.

Maringá had a more tragic story to tell. His wife, Graziela, had been battling pancreatic cancer, and was finally losing the fight. She did not have too long left and her husband was engaged in a permanent vigil at her bedside.

Palmeiras needed just one point in the match against Chape to confirm the *Série A* championship. The game was played in friendly spirits. Under instructions from their *técnico*, the Chapecoense stars played within themselves, ensuring they didn't sustain any injuries, with the much more important event ahead.

Palmeiras won the match 1–0 to seal their ninth *Brasileiro* title. It was the final game in their colours for young *Canarinhos* superstar Gabriel Jesús before he would fly to England and sign for Manchester City in a $30 million deal.

The home supporters stayed and sang their songs of glory. But as the Chape players approached them to applaud their success, they began to chant 'Chape! Chape!' in support for their upcoming final. They even sang the *Canarinhos* songs to let them know that they had the support of the whole nation, and that whilst they would be in the Big Green jersey rather than the famous canary yellow, they would be representing Brazil.

The initial application for *LaMia* Flight 2933 was from São Paulo direct to Medellín, but with a refuelling stop at Cobija, which was almost exactly halfway. When the application was rejected due to the airline not being sanctioned for travel in Brazil, the new flight from Santa Cruz was applied for. *LaMia* thought this shorter flight would not need a refuelling stop, so sent in the application to go direct.

The Bolivian aviation authorities rejected this after their checks confirmed that the *LaMia* plane, a 17-year-old British Aerospace-built Avro RJ85 aircraft had a maximum flight distance on one full tank of fuel of 1,600 nautical miles. The distance between Santa Cruz and Medellín is 1,598 nautical miles. Aviation fuel rules are complicated, but fundamentally, an aircraft needs to carry enough fuel for at least one hour of flying beyond its scheduled journey, to allow for such things as a missed approach, needing to divert to an alternative airport or all manner of other unplanned incidents.

Therefore, the refuelling stop at Cobija was reinstated to the flight plan. The airport at Cobija is merely a small, domestic one. It only stays open through the night for specific prior arrangements and Flight 2933 needed to be there by 7pm or they would miss the scheduled refuelling opportunity.

The flight roster had been formally passed on to the correct authorities. The final Chapecoense party contained a total of 69 passengers. In addition to the 22 players, there were 23 members of club staff, made up of coaches, management and directors. There were also 21 journalists, including Rafael Henzel and Renan Agnolin, who would be covering the huge event for *Rádio Oeste*, and three guests, including Matheus Salori, who was the 21-year-old son of *técnico* Caio Júnior, and the 75-year-old former vice-president of the Brazilian Football Confederation, Delfim Peixoto.

They all arrived at the São Paulo airport in excellent spirits, excited that one more long day travelling was all that separated them from being part of a monumental moment in all of their lives. Only whilst queuing for the check-in desk, did Matheus Salori realise that he hadn't packed for an international flight, so used had he been to flying domestically around Brazil, following his father's teams. He was crestfallen that he would miss out on the whole glorious trip, the match itself especially. But there was no time for him to do anything else but to wish the team luck, shake their hands, give his father a quick hug and say goodbye.

Always joking and laughing, some players taunted him about his silly error, and he giggled with embarrassment as he headed for the airport exit.

For President Sandro Pallaoro, worse news than that came from his wife, Vanusa: Graziela, the wife of his best friend Maringá, had passed away from her cancer. Mortified, he dashed around the airport to see if he could get home to support his childhood friend. But, as usual, there was heavy rain in Chapecó, resulting in the suspension of all flights into the airport. Sandro frantically called Maringá and explained he could not get back. Of course, Maringá had not expected him to do so anyway. He wished the team luck and thanked Sandro for his support and concern; he would see him soon when they returned.

Now down to a party of 68, they climbed aboard the commercial aeroplane, which safely landed on the runway at Viru Viru airport in Santa Cruz three hours later.

Waiting there for them was the *LaMia* Avro RJ85 aircraft, and the nine crew members.

The pilot was the 36-year-old co-owner of the airline, Miguel Quiroga. His co-pilot was 47-year-old Ovar Goytia. Both were Bolivian nationals with exemplary records over many years and several thousand flights.

19

28 November 2016

Viru Viru International Airport
Santa Cruz
Bolivia

4:37pm

The Chapecoense party are waiting eagerly to board their chartered flight. The atmosphere is abuzz with excitement and anticipation. They are all wearing the Chape green and white colours: the management and staff looking smart in bottle-green polo shirts and jeans, the players in white versions of the same shirt, with the bright green ACF logo emblazoned on the breast. They wear the club tracksuit bottoms for comfort. Many plan on sleeping on the flight.

The natural smaller groups begin to splinter off and Tiago, Biteco and Caramelo wander over to the large panoramic window overlooking the runway. They all fall silent as they see the aeroplane that is going to take them to their destiny. It is a spine-tingling moment for the youngsters. Suddenly, Tiago lets out a small excited squeal as he notices a giant version of the same circular green Chapecoense badge that is on their chest, adorning the side of the aircraft's cockpit. *LaMia* have had huge vinyl signs fitted to both sides of the chartered plane, to add to the feel of grandeur and sense of invincibility.

Many others play samba music loudly on their mobile phones, creating a background medley of upbeat sounds, causing many of the party to randomly begin to dance.

Bolivian TV stations have news cameras there, getting interviews with the team that had caused a sensation across the continent. Whilst they speak to striker Kempes, he sees his *técnico*, Caio Júnior and grabs him. He looks into the camera and says Chapecoense cannot lose with this man leading them into battle.

Júnior stays and gives his own interview, in which he explains that travelling via Bolivia gives the team luck, as they had overcome Atlético Junior with a similar itinerary in the quarter-finals.

Danilo had welcomed this year's newcomer and his understudy Jakson Follmann with his typical beaming smile and friendly nature, and he had always remained close friends with the returning Alan Ruschel. The three all live close to each other and have become almost inseparable. Naturally, they are together in the airport.

Ruschel takes a pack of cards with him on all the away journeys, and loves to entertain his friends with tricks. So, in the airport he has Danilo and Follmann gripped to every movement of his fingers, as they stand open-mouthed with glazed eyes, awaiting the trick finale.

When asked if the card revealed was indeed the one they had picked out randomly earlier, the two goalkeepers gasp with amazement before cheering and laughing. Many other players turn to see what the commotion is and Danilo ushers them over. He believes he can replicate the trick Alan has just performed on him. With a far bigger audience, he excitedly shuffles the deck and asks Bruno Rangel to take a card, who ensures the whole crowd sees which one he has picked out.

Danilo takes it back before attempting a series of shuffles and splits with the deck. With the final cut, he asks Bruno if the card revealed is the one he had selected. The audience burst into laughter in unison, as the realisation of failure falls upon the face of the crestfallen *goleiro*. Danilo turns back to Ruschel, and begs 'Mouse' (the affectionate nickname his close friends call him) to show him the trick once more.

Only two members of the party do not feel jovial enough to join in with the dancing and the laughter. President Sandro Pallaoro is mourning the loss of his friend and is deeply concerned about Maringá.

The other is Hélio Neto; the tall defender is anxiously pacing the floor in the departure lounge. Always the friendly father figure, Cadu Gaúcho notices this and asks Neto what is wrong. Neto tells him he is just nervous about the game, and is looking forward to getting some sleep during the flight.

Just as the delegation begins to prepare to board the plane, a crew member makes an announcement: one of the players has requested that he be allowed to retrieve his carry-on bag from the luggage hold, as he had placed it in there by mistake and it contains his video game console, which he intends to use to pass the time on the five-hour journey. As this is a private charter flight the departure time is not as crucial as it would be with a commercial flight. Wanting to keep their highly paying customers happy and content, the *LaMia* staff agree to join him and go in search of the bag. The flight will be delayed by approximately 30 minutes. The players immediately begin to jeer their team-mate, making fun of him and his childish video game obsession until he goes red in the face as he walks toward the exit door with the *LaMia* employees.

Ironic cheers erupt in the waiting area as the crew members and the player return with the treasured item; boarding can now finally begin. As the party enters the plane, all the joyous scenes continue, the samba music is still playing, almost all are laughing and joking. Lots of players pose for selfie photos to put on their social media, allowing their excited supporters to follow their epic journey every step of the way. Some are on the phone to loved ones. Tiago, as ever, is texting Graziele, telling her he loves her and their unborn baby.

The management climb aboard the plane first and are seated at the front, followed by all the journalists who have been instructed to gather together on the seats at the back, allowing all the players to sit together in the middle. That is, with the exception of Alan Ruschel, who sneaks towards the back and sits amongst the journalists. He wants to sleep during the flight, and believes he has more chance of succeeding in this section than with his raucous team-mates.

In the cockpit, the pilots discuss the fact that they are now so far behind schedule, they can no longer make the refuelling stop at Cobija.

Instead, they have two options: attempt the flight direct without refuelling, or go to Bogota International Airport and request clearance to do so en route, which would not be out of the ordinary.

6:18pm

Flight 2933 finally departs from Runway 34 of Viru Viru airport in Santa Cruz. The delay means the plane is setting off in the black of night, as heavy rain falls.

Once in the air, Hélio Neto can try to get some sleep and rest his anxious mind. The card games continue, as does the samba music. Some players join Neto in an attempt to doze the flight away, some are eating, chatting, listening to headphones.

7:20pm

'This is serious,' co-pilot Ovar Goytia tells pilot and *LaMia* co-owner Miguel Quiroga, referring to the fuel problem.

'We have to go up,' Quiroga responds by insisting they increase the altitude of the aircraft, where the air density is lower and therefore less fuel is used during flight.

Flight 2933 is raised to 30,000 feet.

8:37pm

Miguel Quiroga finally admits to his co-pilot he is concerned about the fuel level if they go direct to Rio Negro airport in Medellín. Goytia immediately implores his *capitão* to go for Bogota.

8:48pm

The pilots make contact with Bogota South East Area Control Centre. As is the aviation standard, the pilot introduces his voyage to the controller and declares the altitude of 30,000 feet.

The controller, using the flight reference numbers, knows where the final destination is. The high altitude is enough to convince him that they are flying direct; they should be lower if they aim to land in Bogota.

'You are cleared to Rio Negro via Aruxa, Pabón, Bogota, Bogota-Nirso, Niro's-Rio Negro.'

Assuming the pilots are merely checking their direct route is clear, the controller gives them the checkpoints for the clear and direct route to Medellín. Fuel levels are not his concern nor his responsibility.

Rather than admit the various mistakes he and his own airline have made in getting to this situation, Miguel Quiroga takes the decision to follow the route given by the air traffic controller. They will go direct to Medellín with the very bare minimum of fuel remaining to get there [see map inside reverse cover].

9:03pm

The crew begin their long descent from 30,000 feet to Rio Negro airport.

9:16pm

The pilots request a slight deviation due to the stormy weather ahead. The request is approved.

An aeroplane that had just set off from Bogota to the Caribbean island of San Andres, is diverted to Rio Negro, Medellín, after the pilot reports a mechanical error shortly after departing.

9:31pm

The pilots of Flight 2933 request permission to begin their descent, 53 miles from the destination. The controller tells them to descend to 25,000 feet, and then conduct a circular holding pattern, as the diverted flight with a declared mechanical problem must take priority. The holding pattern manoeuvre is adding distance to the flight. Still, Miguel Quiroga does not tell the controller about the fuel emergency; he knows the moment he declares such a problem, the performance and conduct of himself and his newly formed airline will be profoundly investigated. Having made so many mistakes with the late departure and failure to refuel, such an investigation could lead to a severe criminal prosecution.

Shortly afterwards, the controller instructs the pilots to continue their descent to 24,000 feet and then contact the Medellín approach tower for further instructions.

Pilot: 'Rio Negro, LaMia 2933, good evening.'

Tower: 'LaMia 2933; good evening; descend and maintain [23,000 feet.]'

Moments later, further instructions tell the pilots to descend to 21,000 feet. At the same time the pilots are adjusting their landing gear, the Viva Colombia flight, which has also now confirmed its mechanical problem is fuel related, begins its final approach to Rio Negro.

The *LaMia* pilots nervously begin to perform the holding pattern as instructed.

Alarm after alarm and a plethora of warning lights begin on the control panel inside the cockpit.

In the cabin, Cadu Gaúcho has been to the restroom at the rear of the plane and is walking back to his seat. He notices the journalists chatting over the relaxing Alan Ruschel, who is sat amongst them. He instructs Ruschel to move further forward to allow the journalists to all sit together. He also doesn't want Ruschel overhearing any theories or opinions they may be voicing in their discussions. Alan is comfortable and protests at the instruction. Seeing this, his best friend Jakson Follmann walks to them and urges him to come and sit with him. Cadu returns to his seat.

'Hey, Mouse! Come sit with me,' begs Follmann. 'Let's hear some music. Come on, bro!'

'No, no, I'm gonna sit back here. I want to sleep.'

'Come on, Mouse! Come on!' Follmann insists and will not take no for an answer. Ruschel decides listening to music will be easier than being hounded like this for the remaining 45 minutes of the flight, so moves seats next to Follmann and Danilo.

9:49pm

Whilst performing the second circular pattern, stressed and worried pilot Quiroga finally requests priority landing due to a fuel issue. He desperately does not want to waste more precious fuel on another holding manoeuvre.

Tower: 'LaMia 2933, understand you request priority to land with fuel problems as well, correct?'

Pilot: 'Affirmative.'

Tower: 'Okay. Stand by, I will give you vectors to proceed to the localiser for the approach. Estimate seven minutes to commence approach.'

Commentator Rafael Henzel, sitting at the back of the cabin next to his friend and broadcast partner Renan Agnolin, asks a flight attendant when they will be on the ground. He is told it will be ten minutes, but is alarmed by the worried expression on the face of the crew member.

Back in the cockpit, the enormous severity of what is happening has dawned on Miguel Quiroga, obliterating his previous denial of the situation. Having not yet heard back from the tower with her promise of directions, the panic-stricken co-owner of the airline reopens the communication line.

'LaMia 2933, requesting inbound vectors ma'am.'

'Stand by, I have an aircraft below you on approach. Additionally, they are doing a runway inspection. How much time do you have left on your approach, LaMia 2933?'

'We are with emergency fuel ma'am, that is why I am asking you at once for final course. Request immediate descent.'

The phrase 'emergency fuel' is a signal. This is indeed an emergency. The tower cancels the priority clearance previously given to the Colombian aircraft also suffering fuel problems, and hands approach priority to Quiroga. 'LaMia 2933, can you make a right turn now and begin descent? You have the traffic at one mile below you.'

With Quiroga now resigned to a probable arrest being the best scenario his future holds, the pilots begin a rapid descent and extend their landing gear, and also deploy their aerodynamic brakes in preparation for a rushed and clattering landing.

Tower: 'Captain, you are at ... [21,000 feet]. I need you to descend. Veer right and begin your descent.'

Pilot: 'Negative, we are already starting descent and we are for the localiser.'

Like most of his actions during this flight, this is a reckless one, but Quiroga is now trying to save the lives of all on board his aircraft – although almost all are still blissfully unaware.

9:53pm

One of the four engines of the British-made Avro RJ85 plane fails due to fuel exhaustion. Seconds later, a second engine does the same. Hélio Neto never did properly get to sleep, such was his level of anxiety. He has simply been sat back with his eyes closed for over three hours, just hoping for the flight to be safely over. Suddenly, his large, protruding eyes are very much open.

The source of his restless discomfort had come in the form of a dream which had taken place three nights earlier, the final time he had slept in his own bed in Chapecó, alongside his wife, Simone. He had woken with a start, perspiring all over. He had dreamt the plane would crash, and that the grisly corpses of his friends would lie motionless amongst the wreckage, whilst he walked away almost unscathed, alongside three other passengers.

Such was the vividness of the nightmare that when he had nervously told Simone, she refused to hear anymore, so frightening was the account.

Since then, he had been worried about the flight. Like almost all Brazilians, he is devoutly religious and believed there was a chance it was a warning; a premonition. He had even considered telling people at the club in hope they may consider rescheduling the match. But that would be absurd, to ruin his friends' hopes and dreams. So, he had kept his concerns to himself.

As he opens his eyes on Flight 2933, the stark reality hits him that his deepest fears may be coming true. He remains quiet; the rest of the party are not only unconcerned, but still in a state of euphoria at what they believe their immediate futures have in store for them. They are just putting the two large bumps down to turbulence caused by the stormy weather.

9:55pm

The third engine fails and 14 seconds later, the fourth and final one does the same. On this type of aircraft, the electricity supplies are fed via generators running from engines one and four, both of which have now catastrophically failed.

In the cabin, all the lights go out. The air circulator stops and goes quiet. There is an eery silence, as each and every passenger aboard looks confusedly and worriedly to his friend, colleague, team-mate by his side for reassurance, but is greeted with an expression that merely matches his own.

The plane feels completely still. There is no shaking or rattling. But the rising feeling in their stomachs is telling them the horrifying truth: they are serenely falling towards the ground.

The one passenger not confused anymore is Hélio Neto. He begins to pray, and pray loudly. Almost all of the passengers are soon doing the same: praying to God to save them.

Some of the Chape management seated near the front, begin to scream towards the crew and cockpit for an explanation as to what is happening. No answer is returned.

LaMia Flight 2933 is now in total electrical failure. It disappears from the radar screen of the tower controller. The only hope for the pilots is to perform the spectacular manoeuvre of landing a 'glider'. They need to be close to the runway and need to do it in conjunction with the air traffic controller, who is now working blind.

Pilot: 'Ma'am, LaMia 2933, total electrical failure and, erm, without fuel.'

Tower: 'Runway is clear, LaMia 2933. Rain over the station and fire services are rolled out.'

Pilot: 'Copied. ... Vectors, ma'am. Vectors to the runway!'

Tower: 'We lost radio signal. I can't see you. Report heading now.'

Pilot: 'Heading three-six-zero. Three. Six. Zero.'

Tower: 'I can't see your altitude, LaMia.'

Pilot: '9,000 feet ma'am. Vectors! Vectors!'

Hesitantly and in a sad, quiet and sombre voice, the controller tells the pilots they are still over eight miles away from the runway.

Miguel Quiroga: 'Jesus.'

Tower: 'What is your altitude now?'

There would be no response.

9:59pm

LaMia Flight 2933, travelling at around 150 miles per hour, crashes into the peak of forest mountain Cerro Gordo, Colombia.

The rear of the plane impacts the upward elevation and imbeds due to the ferocity of the landing. The front of the plane breaks off and shoots over the mountain top, finishing almost 500 feet away.

As there is zero fuel, there is no fire or explosion, just a mass of destruction as 40 tonnes of twisted metal and debris gouges its way through forestry.

20

Campeões Eternos II

Jakson Follmann was alive. But he couldn't maintain consciousness due to the unbearable pain. His right foot had been severed completely and his left was hanging by the tendons alone. Every time he came around for a mere few seconds, he heard voices screaming for help, but he couldn't move to assist them. Fewer and fewer grumbling voices were around him every time he woke.

Rafael Henzel was also in a semi-conscious state. Slumped in his aeroplane seat, he repeatedly mumbled 'Renan?', hoping his friend would respond and tell him what was happening. Renan Agnolin did not respond.

Emergency services had been deployed, including helicopters from the Colombian Air Force. But it was the dead of night and thick with fog. It was typically pouring with Chapecó-style rain and the crash site was impossible to access. The helicopters had to land remotely and the rescuers became a search party. The co-ordinates available from the Medellín control tower were only approximate, due to them losing the aircraft from the radar. Therefore, it was over an hour after the crash before a member of the rescue team finally saw the twisted metal panel emblazoned with a giant Chapecoense badge and alerted the rest of the rescuers that finally, they had found the harrowing scene.

Dozens of firemen hurriedly ransacked the wreckage in search of survivors. What they found was one grisly corpse after another.

Alongside policemen and paramedics, they rushed around the whole site, shouting and flashing their torches in hope of any kind of response, be it in movement or an audible cry for help.

Finally, after their yelling and shining lights permeated through his blurred vision and state of shock and horror, Rafael Henzel began to scream at them for help. As they got closer to Jakson, he also regained consciousness and managed to alert them to him. They uncovered him from the wreck and dragged him from his seat, grimacing all the while at the horrifying scenes; the latest being the lowest part of the legs of this survivor.

They could then see the bodies that had been sat closest to Jakson, so checked them for any signs of remaining life. They found it. Alan Ruschel was unconscious but alive in the seat Follmann had relentlessly begged him to take just 30 minutes before the plane shut down. They were in the area which took the impact least catastrophically. Close by, of course, was the third member of their friendship trio: Marcos Danilo Padilha. Danilo, too, had a pulse and was pulled from the debris.

Two of the *LaMia* crew members, female flight attendant Ximena Suárez and male maintenance technician Erwin Tumiri, were also saved.

The firefighters had to carry the bodies of the survivors to the remote area where the helicopters were waiting to fly them to the hospital. The ground was mountainous and thick with mud. The fog was so dense they could not see if their route was clear and they repeatedly slipped on the surface, gashing themselves on large shards of the wreckage.

Alan Ruschel was the first to arrive at the hospital at 2am, shortly followed by Rafael Henzel, Follmann, Danilo and the *LaMia* staff. They were the only six survivors as, at around 5am, the rescue mission was deemed over.

Defensive midfielder Gil was also wrestled from the wreckage alive, but died of his injuries before making it to the hospital.

The remaining passengers were all presumed dead. The mission then turned to one of salvation as the heroes turned their attentions to retrieving all of the possessions for return to the heartbroken, grief-stricken families that were simultaneously being awoken to the devastating news. More helicopters were making their way to Cerro Gordo to take the cadavers to a medical facility in Medellín for identification.

At 5:40am, whilst pulling carry bags and suitcases from the debris, one of the police officers heard something from underneath the felled trees and twisted metal. He called for help from a colleague, who told him there was no chance of another survivor; it had been eight hours since the accident.

'No, no, no. Stay quiet. I heard something.'

They listened closely, trying to filter out the sound of the heavy rain crashing down around them. Suddenly, they both heard a groan and rushed to where it was emanating from. They began pulling tree limbs and branches aside; the adrenaline made throwing the metal pieces away like tossing a frisbee as they desperately tried to uncover one more survivor.

It was Hélio Zampier Neto. The final part of his dream, that he survived and walked away from the disaster alongside three of his friends, was about to come true.

His eyes were rolled into the back of his head. His body and face awash with blood from a multitude of deep cuts. He had severe injuries to his head, thorax, lungs and knees. He had clenched his jaw so tightly in a bid to repel the pain, that his back teeth were broken. The officers had to keep checking he was still breathing, so lifeless was his body as they carried him to a returning helicopter.

Neto became the seventh and final passenger of *LaMia* Flight 2933 to make it to the Colombian hospital alive.

In Chapecó, it is normal to sleep serenely despite the clattering sound of incessant heavy rainfall against your windows, the loud swoosh as every passing vehicle creates a tsunami at the roadside, the gushing of your overflowing gutters pouring into the already flooded sewer grates.

That night was no different, until around 4am. Then bedroom lights across the city began to appear, telephones began to ring, rumour and despair began to spread.

The wives and girlfriends of the players rushed to be by one another's sides, still unaware of the magnitude of the tragedy. Early reports suggested it was just an emergency landing with very few, if any, casualties. Soon after, more details emerged. It was announced that 21 passengers had died, but the majority had survived. Selfishly, but understandably so, each wife, girlfriend, mother, father, son, daughter, brother, sister, relative and friend simply prayed that the next announcement would include their loved one as a survivor.

In almost no time at all, the initial reports of no fatalities had escalated to ones of 'some' survivors. And with that, the despair became intolerable. Every torturous minute that passed took with it their hopes, as the reports became more and more factual, and more and more harrowing.

Mixed reports on the fate of Danilo continued for hours, prolonging the agony of Letícia. Her husband had managed to call her from the hospital despite his agonising injuries, and had told her he loved her and Lorenzo. He was in major distress and his body was utterly broken.

There were nine members of the whole first-team squad who hadn't travelled due to injury, suspension or lack of form. Two of them were legendary veterans Nivaldo and Neném, who were shell-shocked by the news they were being awoken to.

So too were former president Nei Maidana and *Conciliador* Plínio David de Nes Filho. They were woven into the fabric of the club and under normal circumstances, would have travelled with the team. Numb both mentally and physically at hearing the news, Maidana wandered the streets in the lashing rain, before jumping into his car and heading to the stadium. There he found hundreds of relatives and friends of the passengers and supporters of the club, all searching for answers.

The local church too, began to fill, as people desperately prayed to the heavens for good news.

As is the Brazilian tradition on the day a member of your immediate family passes away, Maringá had been sat up all night at home with the body of his wife, Graziela, in her coffin. The family prayed and comforted each other in preparation for the funeral the following day. Already submerged in grief, at 5am Maringá was given the devastating news that dozens of his friends were presumed dead, including his oldest and best friend, Sandro Pallaoro.

The absurdity of it all almost caused him to faint. He describes hearing of the crash as 'insane', and confirms he was 'destroyed'.

But he had to stay strong for Sandro's family. What remained of the two households became united in grief.

At around 7am, the families and friends began to have the fate of their loved ones confirmed. At the stadium, the close friendship group of wives and girlfriends of the players had gathered. All in differing stages of denial, acceptance, anger or grief, they maternally gather around the hysterical Graziele: she was 19 and pregnant and Tiago was her entire life.

The uncertain misery of the family of Danilo, however, continued well into the afternoon, as did the conflicting stories of his fate. It was around 3pm when, in his hometown of Cianorte, his mother, Ilaides, answered the telephone. She had been waiting alongside Danilo's father and sister for news for almost 15 hours. Lacking a sympathetic preamble, the female voice at the other end of the receiver explained she needed to identify a body and wished to do so by describing the three visible tattoos: a Christian cross on the neck, a man and a small boy walking together on the right calf and finally, on the right forearm, a name: Lorenzo. Numb, Ilaides confirmed these unique markings belonged to her son. With that, the conversation ended, plunging the family into despair.

The news soon made its way to Letícia: her husband, Marcos Danilo Padilha, the man with a heart as big as his smile, who had been dubbed *O Deus de Chapecó* due to his heroic goalkeeping exploits, was dead.

The injuries of Rafael Henzel were the least severe: a bad gash above his right eye where a piece of debris or a tree branch had gouged into his face, seven broken ribs, a swollen abdomen and dozens of scratches and bruises were enough for him to call himself the luckiest man alive. He did not require emergency surgery like the three surviving players.

Jakson Follmann had his right leg amputated below the knee; Alan Ruschel was wheeled in for spinal surgery; Hélio Neto was put into an induced coma whilst the doctors decided which of his multitude of serious afflictions needed the most urgent treatment.

The crash was now worldwide news, as tributes poured out from the biggest names and clubs from around the footballing globe on social media. *ForçaChape* became a worldwide expression of support and hope.

Brazil, as a nation, was inconsolably heartbroken and President Michel Temer declared three days of national mourning.

Waking to the horrifying news in a hotel bed in São Paulo had been Chapecó Mayor Buligon, who was, at one stage, listed as a formal passenger of the flight before his busy schedule meant he had to cancel. He immediately got together a delegation containing himself, six doctors and a lawyer, to represent his city and led them on a flight through the storm to Medellín, where a crisis office had already been set up to deal with the disaster.

The Mayor personally identified most of the bodies, to save the families from making the long journey to do that most harrowing of tasks themselves. He knew most of the victims personally. He broke down several times during this nightmarish duty.

He also met with CONMEBOL officials and representatives of the prospective opponents: Atlético Nacional, all of whom were crestfallen. In their run to the final of the competition, Atlético Nacional had also used *LaMia* on multiple occasions and had been aboard the same aircraft that was now a wreck. They understood it could quite easily have happened to them.

Nacional supporters gathered at their stadium to light candles and pray for the victims.

It was decided that during the specific time the match had been due to take place, in the dark evening of Wednesday, 30 November, a tribute would take place. The fans, media and delegates from the game were invited to take part. More than the capacity 40,000 emotionally charged people swarmed into the Estadio Atanasio Girardot; many wore the Chapecoense jersey or at least the green and white colours in which Nacional also play. Strangers wept and hugged. The supporters had joined together to create huge banners to hang around the stadium; one read: 'FOOTBALL HAS NO BORDERS STAY STRONG', whilst another said: 'A NEW FAMILY IS BORN'.

The Nacional players solemnly walked out in black tracksuits, carrying flowers. They were joined by two groups of small children, one dressed in the Chapecoense strip, the other in the kit of Atlético Nacional. Every child carried a white balloon.

Speeches then took place, each as emotional as the last. Mayor Buligon watched on from the side of the pitch, his large, masculine face drenched with sadness. His eyes were blood red and his lip quivered as he struggled to maintain his composure. He wore the same green Chapecoense training shirt the players had worn for the doomed flight.

Finally, the CONMEBOL officials took the microphone. 'The sporting progress of Chapecoense is a clear example of the greatness of South American football, the most passionate sport in the world.

'Due to the tragic events that have occurred, the South American Confederation is in mourning. Our hearts and our prayers are with the victims and their families.

'We won't forget the attitude of Atlético Nacional, and its fans, who asked CONMEBOL to declare Chapecoense the champions of the *Copa Sul Americana*.'

With that announcement, the emotion discharged into a rousing wall of noise as over 40,000 people applauded, cheered and cried in unison. All the children let go of the balloons, which rose into the night sky, representing each one of the tragic victims.

Luciano Buligon allowed himself the smallest of wry smiles, before the tears finally began to tumble down his reddened, wrinkled face.

The heroes of Chapecoense were, and forever would be, *campeões eternos*.

On the Saturday, as the survivors remained in their hospital beds in Medellín, attempting to mentally recover from the news as well as to recover physically, three C-130 Hercules aircrafts belonging to the Brazilian Air Force arrived to collect the caskets of the dead. Fifty of the 71 victims were to be taken to a memorial that afternoon at the Arena Condá. The rest were going elsewhere for private services.

In Chapecó, obviously, the rain was lashing down. But that never stopped the loyal supporters coming to cheer their heroes, it certainly wouldn't stop them coming out to pay homage to them. Almost 100,000 attempted to crowd into the stadium until no more could safely come in. The rest lined the puddled streets for many blocks around it.

Children wore the native Indian headwear in homage to their families' indigenous history. The city over, it was impossible to tell what was rainwater and what was tears. The laundry girls, groundsmen, restaurant workers and cleaners, all of whom adored the players and staff, lined the perimeter of the pitch. Families of the players were on the pitch, carrying photos of their fallen loved one. They were dressed in their prized jerseys. They carried bunches of flowers and hand-written notes from their children.

The then Brazilian President, Michel Temer, was there. He told the press that he believed the heavy rainfall was St Peter crying. The President of FIFA, Giovanni Infantino, was there too, and he gave the final speech of the service, in which he said, 'I want to leave you a hug of solidarity from the world of football and say that FIFA is by your side, not just today but always. *Força Chape*, we are all Brazilians, we are Chapecoenses.'

Also present was ever-popular *Canarinhos técnico* Tite, there to offer his support for all the victims, but particularly his friend and colleague, fitness coach Anderson Paixão. Tite solemnly walked out alongside the coffins.

The groundsmen had prepared the stadium even more carefully than they would for a match day: its exterior was wrapped with a giant black ribbon; flowers and bunting were laid; the goalposts at the end of the field where Danilo performed heroics in the penalty shoot-out against Independiente and his last-ditch block against San Lorenzo just ten days earlier were erected in his honour.

It was eerily silent as soldiers began to carry out the coffins, which were wrapped in plastic to protect them from the pouring rain. Many fans began to sit on the wet concrete steps, unable to watch further; family members began to wail uncontrollably. They were embraced by members of the supporting public. Letícia laid a pair of her husband's goalkeeping gloves in the mouth of the goal he guarded so well, along with his picture.

When the father of Filipe Machado hugged Danilo's mother, Ilaides, she whispered as she sobbed, 'Why did he have to make that save in the last minute?'

A journalist interviewed Ilaides Padilha on the Arena Condá pitch. She could see the pain in his eyes. He too had lost friends and colleagues. Before he could finish asking her a question about her loss, she interrupted him and asked him how he was feeling. His eyes began to fill. 'Can I hug you, on behalf of the entire press?' she asked him before wrapping her arms around him in comfort.

She later said that providing help to others in grief was the only thing keeping her going. She has since founded and now runs a large network support group for bereaved loved ones in Brazil and offers help to thousands of people online and in person.

Her son, Danilo, won the *Craque da Galera*; the *Brasileiro* Fans' Player of the Year award for 2016. She emotionally collected the trophy in his honour at the star-studded ceremony in Rio de Janeiro. The award had previously been won by the likes of Ronaldinho and Thiago Silva.

Associação Chapecoense de Futebol had one match remaining in the 2016 *Série A* programme, at home against Atlético Mineiro. Obviously, this was cancelled. Therefore, Nivaldo never did play his 300th game for Chapecoense, and become the first man to do so. The grief-stricken legend stuck to his vow to retire at the close of the campaign, but pledged to help his beloved team recover once more. He, de Nes Filho and Maringá decided to pour all of their grief and anger into rebuilding the club and the team in honour of their *amigos*.

After a four-decade long association with the club, de Nes Filho finally knew he simply had to become the next president of Chapecoense. Maringá resumed his former role as a vice-president and Nivaldo would attempt to fill the void left by his close friend Cadu Gaúcho, operating between the changing room and the board of directors.

Former president Nei Maidana would also return to assist them and the four of them would need to sign 25 players plus put together a coaching team if the club were to be able to defend their *Campeonato Catarinense* title and subsequently compete in the 2017 *Série A*.

21

Obituarío

Seven of the nine *LaMia* crew members died, including pilot and co-owner **Miguel Quiroga**: the man whose initial greed caused a fuel problem, and whose cowardice in facing the consequences of his actions escalated it to a fuel emergency. His reckless actions are widely regarded as the main cause of the catastrophe.

Only Rafael Henzel survived of the 21-strong journalist delegation aboard the flight. His friend and broadcast partner, who was sat next to him on the plane, **Renan Agnolin**, died.

Amongst that delegation was a former professional player and *técnico*, who had turned to punditry. Mário Sérgio Pontes de Paiva, known simply as **Mário Sérgio**, had played for almost all of the super-power clubs in Brazil in the 70s and 80s. He played and managed Internacional, São Paolo and Botafogo. He even pulled on the legendary yellow Brazil jersey eight times, and did so in the early 80s, when the *Canarinhos* were widely regarded as having the greatest selection of players in international football history. He was 66 years old when he became a victim of the air disaster.

If Alan Ruschel had stayed in his seat near the back when Cadu Gaúcho and Jakson Follmann implored him to sit with his team-mates, there is no doubt he would have been amongst the victims. Instead, he is now back playing first-team football for Chapecoense.

Both guests perished, including the 75-year-old former politician and vice-president of the Brazilian Football Confederation, **Delfim Peixoto**.

Not one individual from the 23 club coaches, management, board members and dignitaries who were sitting at the front survived. They included:

Caio Júnior: Full name Luiz Carlos Salori, he was an experienced and popular *técnico* within the *Brasileiro*. Chape had amassed 37 *Série A* points in his 26 games at the helm, as well as performing miracles in qualification for the *Copa Sul Americana* final. Despite much success as a player and even more as a coach, in the build-up to the final, he said in an interview that this was 'without a doubt ... the best moment' of his career.

His son, Matheus, was supposed to be aboard the doomed flight, but realised he had forgotten his passport at the airport in São Paulo. Caio Júnior was also father to Gabriel and husband to Adriana.

Anderson Paixão: 37-year-old Anderson Rodrigues Paixão Araújo had been with Chapecoense since 2011, when they were in *Série C*. He had played a huge part in turning the players into physically strong athletes and enabling them to keep improving their performance levels, which collectively meant they repeatedly shocked superior teams who underestimated them.

His work meant he was headhunted by representatives of the national team confederation, and he was, at the time of his death, an active member of Tite's coaching staff.

He had followed in the footsteps of his father, Paulo, who was fitness coach for the *Canarinhos* during their 2002 World Cup success. Tragically, in that same year, Paulo had already lost a 25-year-old son, Anderson's brother, due to heart failure.

Anderson Paixão left behind a wife in Ulrike and two children: Jordie and Johann.

Mauro Luiz Stumpf: Affectionately known as Maurinho, Stumpf also joined the Chapecoense family in 2011 at the invitation of his friend, President Pallaoro. He served for almost four years as a volunteer, but his vast contribution to the day-to-day running of the club was much appreciated. So, in 2015, when Maringá left his position as vice-president of football, Maurinho filled the position.

The Chapecoense success on such a tiny budget was largely down to Mauro Stumpf, who left behind wife Daniela and son Alexander.

Jandir Bordignon: 53-year-old Bordignon was one of the original businessmen at the meeting called by Mayor João Rodrigues, and was passionate about the vision presented to him that day. He worked diligently for over a decade in various roles on the board of directors.

Known for his smile and sense of humour, he was hugely popular around the Arena Condá. He was father of two daughters, Letícia and Isabela.

Edir Félix de Marco: The 67-year-old de Marco had been on the Chapecoense board of directors for 30 years, including three terms as president. During his latest spell, between 2006 and 2008, Chape won the *Campeonato Catarinense* and he is credited with laying many of the foundations within the club that allowed it to flourish into the force that it did. In his final act as president, he brokered a deal with Internacional when Chape were to play them in the *Copa do Brasil*, that allowed his team to keep almost all of the revenue, while they were merely a state championship team.

He left behind a widow in Maria and had three adult children.

Cadu Gaúcho: Widely regarded as the football genius behind the rise of Chapecoense, Eduardo Luiz Preuss joined the club as a tenacious midfield player on the recommendation of his friend, Nivaldo. He became a leader on the pitch and turned down a lucrative transfer up the *Brasileiro* to stay loyal to Chape. Shortly after, playing in lowly *Série D*, he sustained a career-ending injury. Jandir Bordignon and then President Nei Maidana repaid his loyalty by offering him a job as a scout and as the connection between changing room and board room.

His ability to spot talent, potential and a wholesome attitude in players is the main reason the team repeatedly excelled beyond expectations. He was soon promoted to a director of football position and was the most respected footballing figure at the club.

Despite achieving so much, he was only 36 years old at the time of the tragedy, and left behind his wife Ana and daughter Gabriele.

Sandro Luiz Pallaoro: President Pallaoro never did make it home to comfort his widowed lifelong friend Maringá. Sandro was another businessman who had been at the 2005 crisis meeting, and had agreed to invest and be on the Chapecoense board.

Just 50 years old at the time of his death, he had been elected 'Entrepreneur of the Year 2015' by the Association of Commerce and Industry of Chapecó.

He and Maringá reluctantly but passionately partnered as president and vice-president respectively in 2010, with the club in *Série C*. They appointed Mauro Stumpf to take charge of the administrative duties and entrusted Cadu Gaúcho to continue to his fantastic work in leading the football department.

In just five years, that management team launched Associação Chapecoense de Futebol into a stratosphere in which they had no realistic right to exist: the small-town *Clube de Futebol* that shot for the stars, but crashed down to earth.

His wife Vanusa, herself responsible for the overwhelmingly welcoming and family atmosphere around the club, would join Maringá in grief.

They had two children, Dhayane and Matheus.

A total of 19 of the Chapecoense first team playing squad that were creating history died that tragic night. They are forever the *Campeões Eternos*:

Canela: Ailton Cesar Junior Alves da Silva was another young discovery from the lower echelons of the *Brasileiro*, the 22-year-old *atacante* from São Paulo had been playing in *Série D* in 2015. He had made just six appearances for the Big Green but was highly regarded and had a bright future.

Ananias: Aged 27, the attacking midfielder Ananias Eloi Castro Monteiro had become the most important offensive player at the club, with Bruno Rangel unable to play every game in his advancing years. The former Palmeiras star played 92 times for Chape in less than two years at the Arena Condá.

Arthur Brasiliano Maia: On a season-long loan from Vitória, the 24-year-old offensive midfielder had made 23 appearances for Chape.

Bruno Rangel Domingues: The biggest idol in the history of Chapecoense. Cadu Gaúcho had long admired Bruno as he forged a journeyman career in the lower leagues, earning minimum wage and battling poverty. He briefly gave up the game and became a banking assistant to earn more money for his family.

When circumstances saw him spearhead the Chape attack in their 2013 *Série B* campaign, his phenomenal goalscoring exploits almost single-handedly enabled them to achieve the impossible dream of making it to *Série A*.

Already 32, he took the opportunity of a lucrative short spell playing in Qatar, but yearned for the Big Green and their supporters, who also yearned for him in return.

Return he did. He struggled to acclimatise to the higher standard and lost his place to Leandro Pereira, and it looked ominously like the comeback would fail and his career would peter out. But when Pereira was snapped up by Palmeiras, Rangel embarked on a second history-making, talismanic period. When Chape *needed* a goal, Bruno delivered it.

His record haul of 81 goals in 162 Chapecoense appearances will probably never be surpassed.

He was 35 at the time of his death and was on the verge of retirement, leaving his wife Girlene and two children, Bàrbara and Daniel, in mourning.

Cléber Santana Loureiro: Instantly installed as *capitão* when he was brought into the club by Vinícius Eutropio at the beginning of the 2015 season, the elegant central midfielder brought a new level of class to the team.

From Recife, he had been successful both there and at Santos before getting the dream move to Europe. He spent four years in Spain playing for Atlético Madrid and Real Mallorca. During that period he scored *La Liga* goals against both Real Madrid and FC Barcelona. He appeared in the European Champions League and won the Europa League.

Another 35-year-old, so close to a happy retirement, he had made 96 appearances for Chape and was husband to Rosangela and father to Arnoldo and Cléber Junior.

Dener Assunção Braz: The 25-year-old left-back had played almost every match in all competitions during his period at the club. He made a sensational 119 appearances in just two seasons for Chape.

Filipe José Machado: Only brought into the club six months before the tragedy, the 32-year-old made 19 appearances for Chape. He was the very definition of a well-travelled journeyman footballer, having played in Brazil, Spain, Bulgaria, Azerbaijan and the United Arab Emirates.

As well as being an experienced defender to provide cover for the first-choice centre-backs, he brought an infectious and vibrant personality to the changing room. He filmed selfie videos of some of the greatest moments of the Chapecoense *Copa Sul Americana* journey, and even did so aboard the *LaMia* plane before it fatally departed Santa Cruz.

Aline is his widow, and they have a toddler daughter in Antonella.

Gil: José Gildeixon Clemente de Paiva, 29, had become the first-choice defensive midfielder after joining Chapecoense from Coritiba at the start of the 2015 season, making 96 appearances.

He was still alive when wrestled from the wreckage, but died from his severe injuries en route to the hospital.

Guilherme Gimenez de Souza: The 21-year-old winger from São Paolo was the youngest victim of the disaster and had played in just 19 first team matches.

Everton Kempes: The charismatic 34-year-old *atacante* was in his second season with Chapecoense and had pulled on the Big Green shirt 53 times, scoring 16 goals. He would entertain his team-mates on long away journeys with his ukulele.

He was married with a son.

Lucas Gomes da Silva: On loan from Londrina, the 26-year-old *atacante* was enjoying by far the best period of his career, most of which had been spent in the lower leagues.

Matheus Biteco: One of three young brothers, all of whom made it as professional footballers, coming through the ranks at Grêmio. The family were firmly poverty-stricken until Matheus, Guilherme and Gabriel made it to the top.

Full name Matheus Bitencourt da Silva, he was also just 21 and had made 24 appearances for Chapecoense on his season-long loan from Grêmio.

Willian Thiego de Jesus: An experienced 30-year-old centre-back who had played for various *Série A* clubs as well as spells in

Japan and Azerbaijan. He had played 84 times for Chapecoense in his two years there and was the subject of interest from Santos, who were willing to offer him a lucrative contract.

Caramelo: Mateus Lucena dos Santos was in his second season of a long-term loan deal from São Paulo. Having spent almost the entirety of that period as a back-up right-back, he had finally made himself first choice in the position in the latter part of the 2016 season. He was just 22 years old.

He gave various accounts of where his nickname, which translates as Caramel, originated, including it being down to his skin colour due to his multiracial ethnicity, but later claimed it was because he was so smooth with the ladies.

Sergio Manoel Barbosa Santos: In his only season with Chape, he had suffered an absence due to a knee injury. The 27-year-old defensive midfielder was just beginning to have a run in the team having spent almost all his career in the lower divisions.

Marcelo: A 25-year-old central defender, Marcelo Augusto Mathias da Silva had just returned from four months out with injury, playing for the first time in the Palmeiras defeat immediately before the tragedy. Due to the injury, he had made just 23 appearances for the Big Green.

Josimar: Instantly installed as first-choice defensive midfielder after signing from Internacional, Josimar Rosado da Silva Tavares was 30 years old and had played 50 times for Chapecoense in his only season at the club.

Tiago da Rocha Vieira: The 22-year-old rapid *atacante* was another miraculous discovery from *Série D* who was making a huge impression after forcing his way into the first team.

A devoted young husband, he had been overjoyed just weeks before the crash when his friends and team-mates played an elaborate trick on behalf of his wife Graziele to inform him of her pregnancy.

He had an amazing future ahead of him, both on and off the football field.

Marcos Danilo Padilha: Tragically, Danilo died from his injuries after he reached the hospital. Despite the excruciating pain, he had managed to call Letícia and tell her he loved her and little Lorenzo.

Only signed on a short-term loan as an emergency *goleiro* at the end of the 2013 season in *Série B*, Danilo's infectious personality and dedication to his craft not only earned him a long-term contract but also the number one jersey for the team that had been promoted to *Série A*.

O Deus de Chapecó became a heroic and immortal figure at the club with multiple-match winning performances, particularly in the epic *Copa Sul Americana* journey.

He had a passionate and unique relationship with the supporters; only Bruno Rangel could rival him for their affections. Both were, still are, and forever will be *Deuses amados* in Chapecó.

22

2017

When Brazilian football cries, the whole football world follows suit.

In honour of not only the victims, but of the Colombian emergency response, medical assistance and legal help and general support, a charity match between Brazil and Colombia was played in Rio which raised $400,000. Rafael Henzel, Alan Ruschel, Hélio Neto and Jakson Follmann were guests of honour.

Neymar Jr. also organised a friendly charity match to be played in tribute to the catastrophe. Amongst the participants that flew to Brazil to take part were Kaká and Gabriel Jesús.

Less than two months after the tragedy, the Big Green finally took to the field once again. On 21 January the rebuilt squad were scheduled to play a friendly match against Palmeiras at the Arena Condá. Of course it was Palmeiras: they were the team who, in the 2013 *Série B,* had first given Chapecoense the belief they could compete with the top clubs; they were the final team Chape had played before getting aboard the doomed flight; they were the current champions of the *Brasileiro*; they had been extraordinarily supportive since the disaster, including offering free loan deals for many of their players.

The match was not important. The emotional ceremony that took place before it was very much the primary object of the day.

Alan Ruschel, Hélio Neto and Jakson Follmann came out onto the field first. Ruschel's gait was slow and rigid, still recovering from extensive spinal surgery. Neto had a patch of hair missing on the back of his head, revealing a huge scar. Follmann was in a wheelchair, being solemnly pushed out by his goalkeeping hero Nivaldo. His right leg was now a stump below the knee, dressed in a beige bandage. He had scars and scabs on all of his skin that was visible. He struggled to hold it together, clearly remembering the joyous times he had been involved with on the same field.

The fans simultaneously sang and cried whilst waving paper origami flowers of the club's badge.

Members of the deceased players' families joined Neto, Nivaldo, Ruschel and Follmann on a presentation stand where they were awarded the *Copa Sul Americana* trophy. The winners' medals were hung around the necks of the wives and children of the *campeões eternos*, whose names appeared on many of the jerseys being worn by their loved ones on the stage, and finally it became too much for Jakson Follmann, who began to sob uncontrollably. He was awarded the trophy, and, straining, lifted it above his head as the crowd let out an impassioned cheer.

Watching on from his radio booth was Rafael Henzel, still nursing seven broken ribs. His most predominant pain, however, came in the form of the empty seat next to him, where Renan Agnolin should have been seated.

The new management team, headed by President de Nes Filho, had put together a coaching team and full playing squad in time to compete in the *Campeonato Catarinense*, which was starting imminently. The football world had come together to support Chape, particularly within the *Brasileiro*. Out-of-contract players clamoured to be part of the rebuilding project, many happy to earn less than they could elsewhere. Clubs gave Chape the first option on players they wished to loan out, and ex-Big Green stars returned to help.

Former *atacante* Túlio de Melo had signed a lucrative agreement with a Qatari club, but Neto sent him a text message whilst still in hospital, pleading with him to come back to Chapecó. Of course, he did.

Just days before his 35th birthday, Neném, still looking in a state of shock, led the team out as *capitão*.

Palmeiras took the lead, but soon after, a high ball was played in towards the goal being attacked by Chape. After a brief scramble, another returning star, Douglas Grolli, brushed it into the goal. The crowd erupted, as did Rafael in his commentary booth. 'Gooooooooooaaaaal!' he screamed. 'My heart overflows! Chapecoense! The team of our heart is reborn with a goal from its past!'

The game finished 2–2, but it was a new team, made up of faces completely unfamiliar to one another.

Chapecoense finally played Atlético Nacional in the *Recopa Sul Americana* in what was the most emotional of all the match-day tributes as fireworks and a big-screen video paid homage to the victims. The dark sky looked haunting as heartache once again surrounded the stadium [see photograph on reverse cover].

Once again, Rafael Henzel, Alan Ruschel, Hélio Neto and Jakson Follmann were paraded in front of the huge and solemn crowd in Medellín. They showed that they were finally recovering, both mentally and physically.

Some things are beyond analysis, description and reason. Associação Chapecoense de Futebol winning the 2017 *Campeonato Catarinense* in front of 20,000 heavy-hearted supporters inside the Arena Condá just five months after the tragedy, is one of those things. It was their second state championship running, and their *Hexacampeonato*, their sixth in total.

The wave of emotion and momentum continued as the new team, led by the grieving Neném, made a stunning start to the *Série A* season. It became traditional that, on the 71st minute of every home match, the announcer would call over the tannoy: 'Our homage to the 71 stars that continue to shine forever for us,' and the crowd would chant, '*Vamos, Vamos Chape!*' for the whole minute. It says much about the heavily Christian community, that they included Miguel Quiroga in their tribute, practising the ultimate forgiveness the Bible teaches them.

In being declared *Sul Americana* champions, they qualified for the *Copa Libertadores* for the first time in their history, and sensationally defeated Lanus in Argentina, who went onto qualify for the final. Chape were eliminated at the group stage by just one point.

As the summer arrived, the survivors were continuing to rehabilitate. Jakson Follmann had a prosthetic leg and was already walking ably on it. He appeared on TV chat shows and spoke of his desire to become a Paralympian. Alan Ruschel and Hélio Neto were training in the hope of playing football again for Chape. Neto was, and still is, aware that he may not achieve that dream. Ruschel, however, was close to becoming fit enough to train again with his team-mates.

Vinícius Eutropio made a romantic return for a three-month spell as *técnico* and guided Chape in some of the most emotional moments of their history.

Top European clubs offered to play friendly matches against Chapecoense in their pre-season, to promote awareness of the tragedy worldwide and to raise funds for the continued rebuilding of the club. Such matches took place against Italian giants AS Roma and, even more sensationally, against FC Barcelona at the Camp Nou.

Ruschel led out the team and played in both matches, even scoring an emotional goal against Roma. He left the pitch on both occasions in floods of tears, and exchanged jerseys with Lionel Messi in Spain.

In October, Follmann married his long-time girlfriend, Andressa. Neto and Ruschel stood next to him as his best men.

Rafael Henzel watched and commentated on all of matches of the Big Green. He also wrote a well-received book, '*Viva Como Se Estivesse de Partida,*' which translates to 'Live As If You Are Going to Die Tomorrow.'

Every goal and every win was dedicated to the fallen heroes. There were moments of guilt, from players, management and supporters, as many didn't yet want to feel joy at a football match.

Remarkably, Chapecoense finished in eighth position in *Série A*; their highest place yet.

In 2018 they would play in the top division for the fifth consecutive season, and they would return to the *Copa Sul Americana.*

Away from the playing field, however, there were no such moments of glory. Bolivia's defence minister declared that: 'What happened in Medellín was murder.'

Immediate blame and anger turned to flight pilot and co-owner of *LaMia* airline, Miguel Quiroga. His clear conflict of interest between adhering to the safety procedures and rules of law as a pilot and his position as a profit-making shareholder of the business led to his horrendous and reckless decision-making during the flight.

The operations of *LaMia* were suspended by the authorities almost immediately as various procedural and criminal investigations began from Bolivia, Brazil and Colombia.

Quiroga's co-owner, Marco Antonio Rocha, was out of the country at the time of the disaster. He never returned. As the investigations uncovered more evidence of institutional misdemeanours by *LaMia*, a warrant was put out for the arrest of Rocha, who became an official fugitive and one of Bolivia's 'Most Wanted'.

It came to light that *LaMia* and Quiroga had carried out the same direct flight between Medellín and Santa Cruz four times. On each occasion, in the same aircraft with the same suicidal amount of fuel. It was reported that, in just the six-month period before the crash, they had completed eight flights with dangerously low fuel levels, including the one carrying the superstars of the Argentina national squad. They were continually playing Russian roulette with their passengers' lives, and it was just a matter of time before tragedy occurred.

CEO Gustavo Vargas Gamboa was arrested and charged with manslaughter, to which he briefly offered to plead guilty in the hope of leniency, before his age and ill health put any trial into question. He has subsequently been placed under house arrest. His son, Gustavo Vargas Villegas, was also arrested. At the time, he had been a top official within Bolivia's civil air authority and was the official that signed off many of *LaMia's* licenses and bureaucratic procedures, facilitating them to operate in Bolivia where they had failed in Venezuela.

In Santa Catarina, the home state of Chapecó, the Brazilian Federal Prosecution Office were pooling investigative findings with those of the Bolivian authorities and evidence came to light that the late Quiroga and missing Rocha were merely figureheads to the actual anonymous owners, a Venezuelan family with links high up in the government.

It also emerged that an air traffic controller who raised red flags before the flight set off on its doomed journey had also fled the country to seek asylum in Brazil, claiming extreme pressure was being applied on her by Bolivian officials and there was even a warrant out for her arrest as Bolivia searched for a scapegoat. CEO Vargas had high-level government ties.

Only Miguel Quiroga truly knows why he made the insanely reckless decisions he did, or what pressures he may have been under to do so.

The VivaColombia flight that had earlier declared a fuel emergency, and was therefore ahead of Flight 2933 in priority for landing, had merely had a malfunctioning fuel gauge.

Late in 2017, Brazilian prosecutors announced that their investigation had failed to show any negligence or improper conduct by the officials of Chapecoense, effectively clearing the club of any wrongdoing in regards to the crash.

Most tragically of all of the bureaucratic fallout, was the fact that *LaMia's* insurance was out of date and invalid at the point of the incident. It had expired due to ongoing contractural infractions, and did not cover them to fly in Colombia anyway.

Miami-based insurance company Bisa, which had provided its services to *LaMia*, had offered $200,000 in compensation to each family, but when the payment was put to a vote by its representatives, they failed to get the unanimous backing they needed. Subsequently, the bereaved families did not receive any meaningful payment and are having to pursue criminal and humanitarian compensation.

In another link to the 1994 World Cup, Romario, the influential hero of Bruno Rangel, has gone on to a political career and is a Senator in Rio de Janeiro, and one of the main figures representing and championing the families in their quest for justice and damages.

No money, though, can bring back what they have truly lost. So many impoverished relatives had been left behind: wives, girlfriends, sons, daughters, mothers, fathers.

Now 29, Letícia had moved back to her home village of Arapongas with Lorenzo, where she had met Danilo whilst he was playing for their lowly semi-professional outfit seven years earlier. They had fallen in love before he took them on to a life the kind of which they could never have dreamt of.

She would try to be tough with herself. It would help her, mentally. She would remind herself that he is gone. But daily, there would be a moment, a smell or a photo, which caused her strength to wilt to nothing and tears to begin streaming down her face.

'Everything changed overnight. All the wives, everyone, had plans: to have another child; to build a house; to travel, with that person. And they were ripped from us. It wasn't like a person being sick, you know? Everyone was good. Everyone was happy. And now, in the night, that person you loved, that you spoke to a few hours ago, was not there anymore.

'It's just unbelievable. They crashed only three minutes from the airport. You have to ask, why? It's hard enough to face that, but then we had that week, waiting, and they landed inside a coffin. At the same airport that they left from, all happy.'

Hardest of all, was explaining to three-year-old Lorenzo why his daddy, his hero, was no longer with them. When they talk of him, and look at his pictures, Lorenzo calls out, '*Campeão!*' Champion.

Letícia was just one of many of the heartbroken widows that felt they had to leave Chapecó. Whilst they understood the club and the community needed to move on and recover, and even to celebrate the victories, for them there was no moving on, there was no recovery, and certainly no celebration. Seeing the stadium full and the joyous, albeit emotional scenes, was just too difficult.

Pregnant Graziele moved back to the town where her and Tiago had met in school. That was Bom Jardim, a couple of hours north of Rio. She had to see a therapist to help her through the grieving process. Her family and friends rallied around her and in January they hosted a party for her to reveal the gender of the baby. She cut the cake and opened it up to expose a bright blue interior. A boy. In unison, her loved ones yelled, 'Tiago!' As they threw confetti over her.

She slept with pictures of her late husband, she listened to voice messages from him that were saved on her phone and she would read the final text message conversations they had, many of which were about baby names.

On 19 July, at 9:25am, Graziele gave birth to a baby boy weighing just over eight pounds. Immediately after delivering him she asked for them to be left alone with just a picture of the father she had packed in her maternity bag.

Of course, she named the boy Tiago.

23

Perder, Ganhar, Viver

The 2018 *Copa do Mundo* was, controversially, held in Russia. The most fancied teams going into the tournament every four years are decided by the equation: recent form + historical results and traditional success at the event + geographical and climatical suitability to the host country.

Italy had failed to qualify for the tournament for the first time since 1958. Defending champions Germany were an ageing team, who hadn't looked quite the same since that fateful day that they destroyed Brazil, both on and off the field, in Belo Horizonte, 2014. Spain were a team in transition, attempting to blood a new generation of young talent. Argentina were the definition of a one-man team in the form of Lionel Messi.

Meanwhile, the *Canarinhos*, under the charismatic and popular *técnico* Tite, had been rejuvenated and were in good form going into the summer, and subsequently, using the equation above, found themselves firmly amongst the favourites. Thoughts of the elusive *Hexacampeonato* were beginning to spread around the country, which would have been unthinkable when they plunged to their lowest ever ebb just four years earlier.

One person that was missing from the Brazilian delegation to Russia was, of course, the late Chapecoense and national team fitness coach Anderson Paixão. They, unlike Argentina, were no longer a team solely reliant on one superstar. That star was, of course, Neymar Jr. But now, he was teamed up in an exciting trio of *atacantes* that contained Phillippe Coutinho, who had just transferred from Liverpool to FC Barcelona for an outrageous fee of around $160 million. Neymar had eclipsed that still, completing a transfer from Barcelona to Paris St Germain in 2017 for approximately $220 million, an astronomical fee that had changed the financial face of the sport.

Completing the attack was young Gabriel Jesús, who had been successful with Manchester City in the English Premier League following his move there from Palmeiras in 2016. He played his final game in the *Brasileiro* against Chapecoense in São Paulo, in the match immediately before they embarked on their doomed journey.

In Alisson Becker they had arguably the best *goleiro* in world football. The ageing but vastly experienced trio of Thiago Silva, Marcelo and Fernandinho all playing at the very elite of European football, meant that Tite could play a team that was not only solid in defence without having to adopt *Era Parreira* tactics, but also was capable of moments of true *Jogo Bonito*.

Had they finally found the balance they had desperately searched for since their 2002 glory?

A solid Switzerland were their first opponents and held a frustrated *Canarinhos* to a 1–1 draw. Two good performances followed, both 2–0 victories over Costa Rica and Serbia respectively.

In the first knockout round, a third successive identical scoreline against Mexico saw Brazil advance to the quarter-final. By now, Germany, Spain and Argentina had all been eliminated and glory was seemingly there for the taking.

Next up was the impressive young Belgian team, who were enjoying their greatest ever golden generation of talent. Many experts and supporters believed the winner of this huge match would probably go on to be World Champions.

Despite the enormous distance, the city of Kazan swarmed with supporters in the famous yellow jersey. Once again, the 200 million population of Brazil came to a standstill. They hoped. They prayed.

Brazil began the match well, dominating possession and forcing Belgium to defend deep. From a corner kick delivered by

Neymar, Thiago Silva had the goal gaping from just two yards, but mistimed his attempted side-footed finish and the ball clattered against his thigh and agonisingly up into the air and onto the crossbar.

Moments later, it was Belgium who had a corner kick, and an almost identical cross was swung in. Fernandinho seemed to have the relatively simple job of heading it clear, but he too got his body shape and timing wrong and the ball ricocheted off his shoulder and past Alisson, to put Belgium, who hadn't really created a chance, into the lead.

Showing great attitude, Brazil continued to press forward and endeavoured to score the equalising goal. The ball spent almost all of its time in and around the Belgium penalty area, until giant Manchester United *atacante* Romelu Lukaku came back to collect it. Using his pace and power he carried the ball forward, the small midfielders of the *Canarinhos* powerless to stop him. Into the Brazil half he went before playing a short pass to his advancing compatriot, another star of the English Premier League, Kevin De Bruyne. Knowing his dangerous talents, the defenders continued to retreat towards their own goal. Once within 25 yards of his target, De Bruyne unleashed a venomous, spectacular low drive across helpless *goleiro* Alisson and into the bottom corner of his goal.

Despite being the better team, a couple of uncharacteristic mistakes and a sublime piece of skill from one of the premium players in the world, saw Brazil two goals behind and looking certain to be eliminated.

Give in, they did not. In the second half they created chance after chance. They hit the crossbar, they struck the upright post. They found Belgium *goleiro* Thibaut Courtois in inspired form.

With less than 20 minutes remaining, Tite substituted Renato Augusto on in place of Paulinho. Just three minutes later the change looked like a move of genius as Coutinho gloriously lifted a perfect pass into the path of Augusto, who guided the ball past Courtois with his head to give 200 million people hope.

They continued to push forward and the football world began to will the ball into the goal for the eternally popular Samba Boys.

But, heartbreakingly, time ran out for them.

'HEXIT', was the clever headline in *O Globo* the following morning, as they highlighted the result which meant *Hexacampeonato* would have to wait at least four more years.

Underneath, read the subheading: *'Derrotada pela Bélgica por 2 a 1 num jogaço em Kazan, a seleção pode continuar sua recuperação sem sair do zero.'* (Defeated by Belgium by 2 to 1 in the game in Kazan, but we can recover without starting from zero).

The press and public alike took the loss better than ever before. There would be no dramatic overreaction.

Ending a tradition spanning 40 years and seven consecutive coaches that had instantly been fired after returning home from the *Copa do Mundo* trophy-less, the Brazilian Football Confederation assured Tite that his job was safe and he could continue with his project and philosophy.

In early 2019, with the country preparing to host the *Copa América*, the Brazilian Football Association issued another statement reiterating that, regardless of the result in the competition, Tite's post would still be secure.

A long 36 years after Carlos Drummond de Andrade's poem implored the country to accept footballing defeat in a reasonable manner, it had finally happened. But it had taken a disaster the scale of the Chapecoense catastrophe to give them the perspective they needed.

Bruno Rangel Domingues and Marcos Danilo Padilha may never have played for their *amado* country, but they had represented it passionately and glitteringly in the amazing *Copa Sul Americana* triumph; and in their tragedy, they had finally taught the whole nation how to simultaneously Win, Lose and Live.

Perder, Ganhar, Viver

Claudio Taffarel celebrates as Roberto Baggio's missed penalty awards Brazil the 1994 World Cup.

Era Parreira begins as Romario (with trophy) and Dunga (captain) celebrate.

Sergio, the author, Si and Jono inside the Maracanã.

With *Série A* survival assured, Danilo gives way to his mentor: The Eternal Nivaldo.

Danilo saves the final penalty in the epic *Copa Sul Americana* shootout against Independiente ...

... and his team-mates, led by Bruno Rangel, rush to celebrate with him.

When they reach him, they embrace.

(Top L-R) Danilo; Caramelo; Santana(c); Thiego; Neto; Josimar; (Front L-R) Kempes; Gil; Tiago; Ananias; Dener line up for the semi-final second leg against San Lorenzo at the Arena Condá. Only Neto was alive ten days later.

COPA SUDAMERICANA 2016

Before: The *LaMia* Avro RJ85 aircraft prepared for the Chapecoense delegation.

After: The aeroplane wreckage in the mountains of Cerro Gordo.

Hélio Zampier Neto is carried away from the crash site by paramedics.

The Big Green supporters show their emotional support upon hearing the news.

All the coffins are dressed and blessed in preparation for their flight home; this is the one containing vice-president Mauro Stumpf.

Brazilian Air Force troops carry out the coffins at the rain-soaked Arena Condá.

Fans sob uncontrollably at the memorial.

The Chapecoense mascot pays tribute, whilst behind him is a flag made by supporters to thank Colombia.

Brazilian head coach Tite
waves as he gives his support
to the city.

Letícia and members of Danilo's family struggle to hold it together as they pay tribute to him.

Nivaldo supports the three surviving players at the *Copa Sul Americana* trophy ceremony before the first game back for Chapecoense.

The children that have lost their fathers lift the *Copa Sul Americana* trophy.

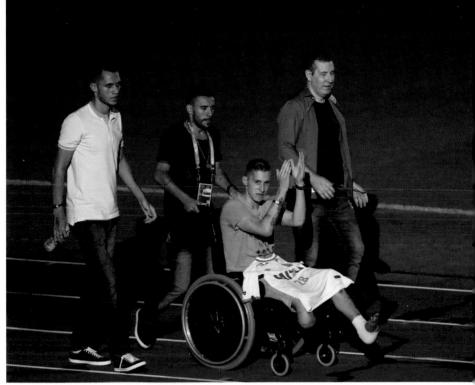

The three playing survivors and Rafael Henzel parade in front of the crowd.

Plínio David de Nes Filho (right) and Maringá (centre) present Italy legend Francesco Totti with a memorial shirt as a thank you for the charity game Roma played against Chape at the Stadio Olimpico.

Alan Ruschel, supported by Nením, captains Chape against FC Barcelona at the Camp Nou.

Vinícius Eutropio joins Follmann, Neto and Ruschel on the pitch in Barcelona.

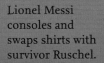

Lionel Messi
consoles and
swaps shirts with
survivor Ruschel.

Henzel, Neto, Ruschel and Follmann are looking healthier at the Recopa match against Nacional.

Epílogo

Associação Chapecoense de Futebol got to their third consecutive *Campeonato Catarinense* final in 2018, but lost their two-year stranglehold on the trophy, losing by two goals to nil against Figueirense.

Still being led off the field by now 72-year-old President de Ncs Filho and on the pitch by 36-year-old Neném, the strain finally began to show. Chape struggled in the 2018 *Série A*, and spent almost the whole campaign in the *rebaixamento* zone. They went into the final game of the season needing to beat the mighty São Paulo at the Arena Condá in order to avoid, after the most turbulent five years of any *Clube de Futebol* in the history of the sport, a return to *Série B*.

Into the second half, the match was goalless, leaving the 20,000 Chape supporters in the stadium in the familiar, torturous state they had become so accustomed to. They needed a goal. Even more ominously, in contrast to almost all of the times the Big Green had shocked the world by grinding out their sensational results, it was a glorious day in Chapecó. There was not a cloud in the sky and the low, bright sun cast large shadows on the turf, and the fans, clad only in their Chapecoense jerseys rather than a clear plastic rain mac, had to shield their eyes from the glare.

With just 20 minutes remaining, the ball was with Big Green right-winger Canteros, who crossed it into the penalty area, hoping to seek out the lone *atacante*, who was surrounded by São Paulo defenders. That *atacante* was Leandro Pereira. The same Leandro Pereira who, as a 23-year-old in 2014, had replaced the misfiring

Bruno Rangel and, in a blistering four-month spell, scored ten goals to save Chape from certain *rebaixamento* in their first campaign back in *Série A*. He had been another discovery of the Cadu Gaúcho regime and had subsequently earned himself a prosperous move to Palmeiras. Despite continuing with a respectable goalscoring rate, he never managed to make himself a first-choice star at his new club and went onto spells with Club Brugge in Belgium before returning to the *Brasileiro* with Sport Recife. He had lost his way a little bit and his career hadn't blossomed as it looked like it would. But for the 2018 *Série A* season, he would return home. In the three years he had spent away from Chapecó, he had scored just 17 goals. Already since his return, he had scored ten top-division goals for Chape and now he desperately wrestled with the São Paulo defenders in a bid to get to the crossed ball and save his club from relegation for the second time.

'Gooooooooaaaaaaaaaaaal!' screamed Rafael Henzel from his commentary position. 'My heart overflows with happiness! The Big Green will not fall! Leandro Pereira heads in the middle of the defence of São Paulo and makes all of our hearts overflow with happiness!

'Leandro; Leandro Pereira, you do not know the joy you give to the Chape supporter!

'Firm. Strong. Reassuring the heart of this passionate fan of the Arena Condá.

'It's the green machine that will never fall!'

The usual and now famous result of Chapecoense using *Era Parreira* tactics when they absolutely needed the victory at the Arena Condá was 1–0; and they achieved it again to further extend their epic and legendary spell in the top league of the *Brasileiro*.

The celebrations were long, familiar and emotional.

Amongst the substitutes that day and most emotional of all were Neném and Alan Ruschel. During the season, Odair *'Neném'* Souza had finally done what his friend Nivaldo so agonisingly failed to do: he had become the first Chapecoense player to make 300 competitive appearances for the club. He also scored his first goal in five years. Since joining them over a decade earlier with the club outside the national leagues, together they had achieved four promotions, won three *Campeonato Catarinense* titles, a *Copa Sul*

Americana championship and miraculously stayed in *Série A* for a sixth successive season. He had never suffered a *rebaixamento* but had endured the most traumatic catastrophe in sporting history.

Once the dust had settled on another dramatic season's end, Neném announced his retirement.

Alan Ruschel had made 15 first team appearances during the 2018 campaign and is widely expected to be back as first-choice left full-back for the 2019 season.

Hélio Neto continues to work tirelessly towards a comeback and has been officially named as a member of the Chapecoense first team squad for 2019.

Jakson Follmann is working as an ambassador for the *Clube de Futebol* and is still training towards a dream of becoming a Paralympian.

Away from the football, however, the recovery is slower. Despite all the arrests, no firm prosecutions have yet been made as court cases are delayed and continue to encounter various legal problems.

Similarly, the bereaved families' quest for compensation carries on excruciatingly through appeal processes and international court proceedings.

In 2018, representatives from Chapecoense and from the friends and families of the victims set up the AFAV-C: *Associação dos Familiares e Amigos das Vítimas do Vôo da Chapecoense* (Association of Relatives and Friends of Chapecoense Flight Victims), which is working with the authorities and politicians, to help provide financial support to those that need it.

Acknowledgements

I am very grateful to everyone who helped me with this project, and would like to start by thanking the team at Pitch Publishing. For an author to get his or her first manuscript taken on by a recognised publishing house is uncommon in the modern world of self-publication and, well, Amazon. But their guidance, support and expertise were invaluable in enabling me to produce the best possible product I could.

At various times during the process I repeatedly felt I simply could not find all of the information I required. *Sports Illustrated* had published a fantastic article by S.L. Price, 'The Fairytale and the Nightmare', as did ESPN in 'Eternal Champions' by Sam Borden. I'd like to thank those two writers and their articles for initially piquing my interest and turning it into an obsession that led me to follow the dream of writing a book, but also for providing the seeds of information which I endeavoured to grow.

After my well of English language resources ran dry, I contacted Sergio, my *amigo* from my time in Brazil, and asked him to search for answers to my questions in his native language of Portuguese and translate them back to me.

What he went on to do was far beyond what I had hoped. We conversed online weekly throughout the year of 2018 and he would tirelessly search for information he thought I may need. He would send me translations of news articles, videos which he applied English subtitles to, using his exemplary technological skills, and an endless stream of thoughtful, entertaining and occasionally hilarious anecdotes; some more relevant to the subject matter than others!

Our acquaintance turned into a solid friendship and I cannot possibly thank him enough for his contributions towards this book; it simply would not exist in this form without him.

His name is Sergio Marcio Furtado Valeriano, a gentleman of the highest regard. He was there when this journey began during my trip to Brazil in 2014; as were my two great friends Si and Jono. They too have my eternal gratitude for being such brilliant company on that fantastic adventure.

I would like to thank Eric Michael Becker, who penned the translation of the famous Carlos Drummond de Andrade poem: *Perder, Ganhar, Viver* and Fernando Rinaldi of Brazilian publisher *Companhia das Letras*, who gave me permission to use the classic work in this project.

I tried contacting various people connected, directly or indirectly, to the decade-long adventure I wanted to cover. The only one who really assisted me, and he did so with charm and enthusiasm, was former Chapecoense *técnico* Vinícius Eutropio. He sent me text message after text message and newspaper clippings he thought may be useful to me. He even sent me some personal photographs of his; the final one was him with Cadu Gaúcho, Sandro Pallaoro and Mauro Stumpf; in the text that accompanied it, he wrote that he lost many friends in the disaster.

I kept the project secret for a long time, mostly for fear of failure. But the encouragement of those of you I had the courage to tell (and bore) with it all was absolutely invaluable, especially when I had crises of confidence. So, as well as the aforementioned Sergio, thank you to my brother Martin, sister Aisling, Mam, Dad and best-buddy Martyn.

One name missing from that list is that of my wife. It was she who first told me she believed I had a talent for writing. When I told her I was about to embark on the project, I said it would be extremely time intensive and that may mean less meals out, less DIY and less gardening. She simply insisted I do it, and even bought me all the writing materials I could need for Christmas, as I was embarking on the journey at the end of 2017. So Nicola May Bell, the biggest thank you of all goes to you and *only you*.

Selected Bibliography

Books
Nedel, Marco Aurélio, *Chapecoense: O Triunfo da Ética*
Rizzica, Lucio, *Proprio come una Cometa*

Articles
Price, S.L., *The Fairytale and the Nightmare* (Sports Illustrated)
Borden, Sam, *Eternal Champions* (ESPN)
O'Mahony, Conor, *The Terrible Truth Behind the Chapecoense Tragedy* (Pundit Arena)
One year after the Chapecoense plane crash, suspicion of foul play (The Brazilian Report)
Pazini, Gabriel & Edwards, Daniel, *Out of the ashes: The incredible story of Chapecoense's resurrection* (Goal)
Tomorrow Belongs to God (The Players' Tribune)
Not Enough Fuel: The Disgusting Truth About LaMia Flight 2933 (Fear of Landing)
Ferreira, Leonardo, *Rangel turned his back on big money to make history with Chapecoense* (ESPN Brazil)
Chapecoense plane crash: The victims, the survivors and those left behind (BBC)
Chapecoense striker had just found out he would be a dad (ABS-CBN Sports)

Websites
Acervo.oglobo
Chapecoense
Corinthian1882
Corinthian-casuals
Soccerway
Wikipedia

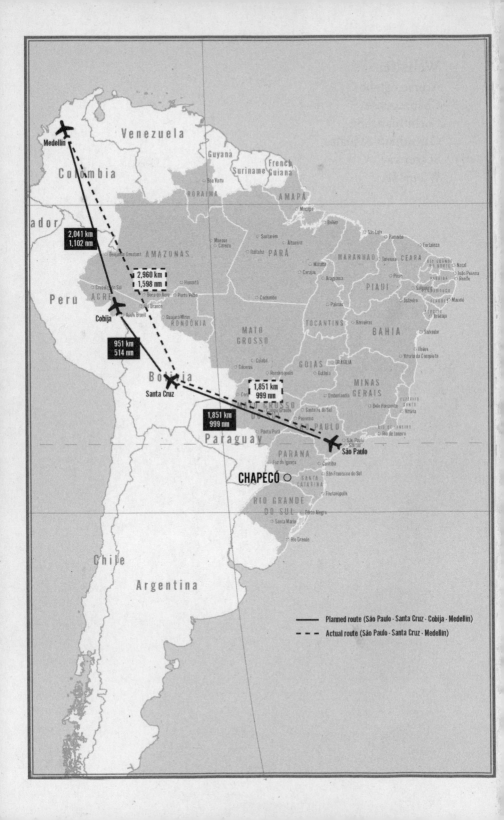

Venezuela

Guyana

Suriname French
Guiana

Medellín

Colombia

ador

2,041 km
1,102 nm

AMAPA

RORAIMA

Macapá

Belém

São Luís Parnaíba

Manaus
Careiro

Santarém

Altamira

Itaituba

PARÁ

Fortaleza

MARANHÃO

Teresina CEARÁ

Piauí

Natal

João Pessoa

Recife

Maceió

Aracaju

Peru

2,960 km
1,598 nm

Humaitá

Boca do Acre

Porto Velho

Crazeiro do Sul

ACRE

Assis Brasil

Cobija

Rio Branco

951 km
514 nm

Guajará-Mirim

RONDÔNIA

Cachimbo

MATO
GROSSO

Palmas

TOCANTINS

Barreiras

BAHIA

Salvador

Ilhéus

Vitória da Conquista

Cuiabá

Cáceres

Rondonópolis

GOIÁS

Goiânia

BRASÍLIA

MINAS
GERAIS

Bolivia

Santa Cruz

1,851 km
999 nm

Uberlândia

Belo Horizonte

Vitória

1,851 km
999 nm

Santa Fé do Sul

Campo Grande

PAULO

Panorama

São Paulo

São Paulo
São Sul

Rio de Janeiro

Paraguay

Ponta Porã

PARANA

Foz do Iguaçu

Curitiba

CHAPECÓ ○

São Francisco do Sul

SANTA
CATARINA

Florianópolis

Chile

RIO GRANDE
DO SUL

Porto Alegre

Santa Maria

Argentina

Rio Grande

———— Planned route (São Paulo - Santa Cruz - Cobija - Medellín)

- - - - Actual route (São Paulo - Santa Cruz - Medellín)